Fatin Al-Tawil

European Fiscal Intervention to ameliorate Palestinian HE

Fatin Al-Tawil

European Fiscal Intervention to ameliorate Palestinian HE

The Impact of Erasmus+ projects on Enhancing Palestinian Higher Education

Noor Publishing

Imprint

Cover image: www.ingimage.com

Publisher:
Noor Publishing
is a trademark of
International Book Market Service Ltd., member of OmniScriptum Publishing Group
17 Meldrum Street, Beau Bassin 71504, Mauritius
Printed at: see last page
ISBN: 978-620-0-77891-8

The Impact of International Higher Education Aid on Promoting Intercultural Communication: Case Study of Erasmus+ in Palestine

By

Fatin Ibrahim Ali Al-Tawil

May-22-2020

Dedication

I dedicate my research to my parents, brothers and my five angels.

My idol, I promised you that I will one day walk in your shoes and here I am, dearest father.

I grant you my first step to success, promising to vanquish all the hurdles since the sky is my limit.

My haven, your endless support and belief elevated my aspiration to limitless objectives and here I am, mother, climbing the ladder of success to reach my utmost satisfaction.

Precious brothers, my success is due to your support. You have taught me determination and here I am determined, focused and ready to explore the ambiguous world.

My precious five angels, my luck in life, my dearest children, to you all, to each one of you I dedicate my success to be a reflection to your coming success. I believe in each one of you, go ahead and flourish. Dreams definitely come true once we give all our strength to it. Believe in yourselves, a message that I transfer to all. Thanks for your endless support.

Abstract

Erasmus+ programme is the biggest mechanism in funding higher education institutions in Palestine and elsewhere. It is the European Union programme that supports individuals and organizations as well. With an allocated budget of 16.5 billion euros, Erasmus+ has modernized, innovated and ameliorated the Higher Education. Furthermore, it has enhanced the governance and the internationalization of HEIs. Due to the lack of related studies conducted in Palestine on the importance and impact of Erasmus+ programme on higher education despite its substantial funding in this domain, the researcher has conducted this study to see the implications of this aid on the Palestinian universities.

Purpose: The study aims at investigating the impact of Erasmus+ aid on enhancing intercultural communication in Palestine. Moreover, the researcher inspected the extent of Erasmus+ impact in helping in cooperation and intercultural communication. The researcher also investigated the impact of the Erasmus+ projects in bridging the socio-cultural gap between the higher education system in the Palestinian and the European institutions, and the projects' contribution in promoting the cultural knowledge in Palestine and Europe yielding sustainable cooperation. Finally, the researcher measured the impact of cultural interaction among the higher education institutions at the individual, institutional and national level.

Design/ Methodology/Approach: The researcher used the qualitative descriptive content analysis to sort and interpret all the gathered documents and templates that are related to Erasmus+ International Credit Mobility, ICM and the Capacity building in higher education CBHE projects. Moreover, the documents describing the impacts of Erasmus+ projects were coded into categories. The researcher described the impact of

Erasmus+ on various targeted Palestinian universities which participated in Erasmus+ projects. Furthermore, the researcher used the section of "Impact" in EACEA's template form while accumulating the data from Palestinian universities to describe the impact of Erasmus+ projects at three levels: - the individual level, the institutional level and the national level.

Sample of the study: The researcher used the purposeful sampling to generate beneficial information through selecting and choosing seven of Erasmus+ projects that have impact and are conducted from 2015-2019 by various Palestinian Universities such as Birzeit University, Hebron University, An-Najah National University, University College of Applied Sciences, Islamic University of Gaza, Al Azhar university and Bethlehem University. The sample represents 41% of the accumulation of Erasmus+ projects which are 50 CBHE projects and 2200 ICM mobilities with a budget of 44 million euros. The sample consists of the accumulated documents and the interviews that the researcher has conducted between the coordinators of Erasmus+ CBHE projects and the director of National Erasmus Office in Palestine.

Findings: From the analysis performed, it was found that Erasmus+ projects had impact at three levels. The main result at the individual level is that many graduates worked at the governmental and non-governmental sectors including the Ministry of Higher Education and Scientific Research after the termination of their studies. On the other hand, at the institutional level, new Master's programmes were established in Palestine for the first time such as: intellectual property, forensic computing and cyber-crimes. Lastly, at the national level, the governance of the universities was improved due to the involvement of the Ministry of Higher Education and Scientific Research. This has shown that Erasmus+, through its projects and with the cooperation of the Palestinian universities and the interference of the Ministry of Higher Education and Scientific Research, has succeeded in enhancing intercultural communication between Palestine and the regional countries in Europe and the Middle East.

Recommendations: With regard to the results of the study, the researcher recommended to invest more in Erasmus+ to build the capacities of the Palestinian universities. In addition, another recommendation was to expand Erasmus+ programme in order to cover different sectors.

Contents

List of Tables

List of Charts and Graphs

List of Abbreviations

ANNU	An-Najah National University
BU	Bethlehem University
BZU	Birzeit University
CBHE	The Capacity Building in the Field of Higher Education
DAAD	The German Academic Exchange Service
EACEA	Education Audio Visual and Culture Executive Agency
ERASMUS+	European Region Action Scheme for the Mobility of University Students

HEIs	Higher Education Institutions
ICM	International Credit Mobility
METHODS	Modernization of Teaching Methodologies in Higher Education
PBL	Problem Based Learning
PENS	Pathway in Enterprise Systems Engineering
PIC	Participant Identification Code
ROMOR	Research Output Management through Open Access Institutional Repositories in Palestinian Higher Education
TAP	Transforming Assessment Practices in Higher Education in Palestine.
UNIGOV	Improving Governance Practices and Palestinian Higher Education Institutions
UNIMAS	Universiti Malaysia Sarawak
USAID	United States Agency for International Development

Chapter One

Introduction

Chapter One

Introduction

1.1. Preview

This chapter demonstrates the significance of the international higher education to the world in general and Palestine in particular. It also displays types of international higher education funding to Palestine. Furthermore, this chapter sheds the light on Erasmus+, the European funding programme in Palestine that aims through its synergies at ameliorating, reforming and upgrading students, staff and curricula in the higher education institutions. In addition, the remaining components of the chapter consist of the statement of the problem, the aim and objectives of the study, the questions of the study, the significance of the study, the limitations of the study, and the operational definition for the main terms used in the study.

1.2. Introduction

After World War II and due to the industrial revolution, education has been affected. An enormous growth of the need of skilled educated workers urged to modify the education system and kind of curriculum to convoy the globalized need of development (Penprase, 2018). To state the matter differently, due to the mass growth of the economy and the accelerated need of well-educated students to cope with this development, education has been attainable to all segments of society (Power, 2014). Therefore, students pursue their higher education to compete with the necessity of globalization. Due to this mass growth of students seeking to complete their tertiary education, states alone cannot afford to educate these numbers of students; hence, higher education tends to internationalize their holistic system. In addition, internationalization of higher education requires the adequacy of student, staff and curricula. This can be done through utilizing new innovative educational approaches used in international universities that mainly depend on ameliorating quality in higher education in order to gain sustainability, social equity and economic security among all segments of society (Mense, Lemoine, Garrestson & Richardson, 2018). Moreover, through internationalization of higher education, integration is achieved and that is by student mobility and employability abroad and also by fostering cooperation with universities. Optimal goals are implemented at different levels, individual, institutional, national and international (Ho, Lin & Yang, 2015).

Palestine, as a country, complies with the international objectives of higher education. According to the Ministry of Higher Education and Scientific Research, Palestine has 49 higher education institutions involving 214,000 students distributed in different universities with different specialties (Ministry of Higher Education and Palestinian Scientific Research, 2019). What distinguishes Palestinian higher education institutions from others is that it has a public concept which facilitates "education for all". This exactly mirrors the World Bank strategy goal that aims at gaining sustainable development by improving the quality of education for all. This, in return, generates a continual learning process that lasts up till 2030 (World Bank, 2019).

The Palestinian Ministry of Higher Education and Scientific Research has a universal vision implemented through its scientific research that convoys the global development. It supports higher education institutions to trigger the spirit of competitiveness among its students. Moreover, the Ministry of Higher Education and Scientific Research fosters uniqueness and innovation in scientific research through enhancing creative analytical thinking and problem- solving skills in order to adapt to the advanced technology and requirements of this era. Furthermore, through its endeavors, the Palestinian Ministry of Higher Education and Scientific Research aims at improving the outputs of higher education institutions. According to the World Bank, higher education is a means that enhances growth, lessens poverty, and engages in multinational prosperity (World Bank, 2017). To assure sustainable development, the ministry of higher education and Scientific Research fosters mutual networking cooperation between Palestinian and international institutions to promote "inclusive and quality education for all" were quality education is permissible to all Palestinians. Palestinians receive funding from different countries such as the United Kingdom, the United States etc. Moreover, in Palestine, technical and vocational institutions have the same importance as other higher education institutions since they provide participants with the skills and competencies necessary for any recruitment. Through these synergies, Palestinians get a unique education that is based on high quality, innovative skills. Through mutual cooperation and vis-vis contact, they become culturally competent (Ministry of Higher Education and Scientific Research, 2019).

However, according to the United Nations conference on Trade and Development (UNCTAD), Palestine is under a continuous fiscal deterioration that raises their poverty and unemployment levels (United Nations conference on TRADE AND DEVELOPMENT, 2019). Therefore, and since Palestine has been always under occupation, Palestinians do not have any control over their economy and resources. Likewise, Palestinians lack a complete control over their education system and have limited fiscal resources to proceed on developing their educational system. These limited financial allocations urge Palestinians to engage in international cooperation and depend upon international financial aid to elevate the education process and reduce poverty and unemployment levels. This is because, according to Heyneman and Lee, "the higher an individual's level of education, the less likely they will be unemployed or in poverty" (Heyneman & Lee, 2016, p. 9). Therefore, the researcher provides some examples of multilateral financial assistance donated to the Palestinians that helps upgrade their individuals' educational abilities and enrich their knowledge and awareness of the donors' cultures resulting in influencing their behavior, lifestyles, and ideas.

As an example of international aids programs, HESPAL, an international higher education scholarship in Palestine, has been established by the British council in 2011(Rantisi, 2015). It offers international standards and good quality of education to Palestinian staff who work at Palestinian universities in order to qualify staff and improve university education. Successful candidates of this scholarship are offered Master's or PhD scholarships, but after their completion of studies, they must come back and serve at their home universities. Forty or more grants are distributed among Palestinian universities to upgrade their academic levels. The partner universities are accountable for the Palestinian staff fees whereas the British council is responsible for other living expenses (HESPAL, 2019)

Another example of financial aid is the Chevening Scholarship that offers Master's scholarships. A lot of Palestinian alumni have engaged in this scholarship and gained benefits as a result. Through their interaction with others in transportation and other daily activities, they have come to be tolerant of other cultures (Chevening, 2019). It is a fully funded global scholarship established in 1983 and granted to outstanding individuals who have completed their Bachelor's degree at Palestinian universities and are willing to complete a one-year Master degree at any UK university. The applicant must have a two year of work experience before applying to the grant and must come back to his country after the award duration is over. He/ she must stay at least two years in their country before thinking to pursue their further studies in the UK. In general, the Chevening Scholarship aims at creating strong leaderships by building strong relationships and strengthening international development with other cultures including the UK's (Enfield, 2019). It also seeks to improve individuals professionally and academically.

Furthermore, the United States Agency for International Development (USAID), established in 1961 in the United States by John Kennedy, consists of foreign assistance organizations and programs that are responsible for promoting social and economic development. They seek to decrease poverty in the United States and the developing countries. USAID assistance tackles the educational system as well. As for Palestinians, USAID has helped the ministry of higher education and Scientific Researchto ameliorate their higher education system through introducing new approaches and methodologies to promote sustainable development and quality of education. It has also helped in shaping and designing educational programs to be implemented in Palestine. On the other hand, through its projects, the USAID tends to train the youth aged 14-29 to have strong leadership skills that enable them to think critically while problem-solving. Graduates can also pursue to complete a one-year Master's degree and come back to develop their country (Education Development Program, 2014).

In addition, the Fulbright Scholarship, founded by the American Senator J. William Fulbright in 1946 and funded by the government of the United States, provides 8000 grants annually. The aim of this scholarship is to increase cross-cultural relations between the United States and other cultures to maintain peace, mutual understanding and benevolence through the students' educational exchange scholarship programs (Perna et al., 2014). In the case of Palestine, students enroll to study a two-year fully granted Master's program at any American university. The applicant must have a year of work experience prior to applying for this grant. He / she must be academically excellent, have the leadership qualifications and can easily adapt to the American culture (Fulbright Foreign Student Program, 2019).

Moreover, the German Academic Exchange Service (DAAD), established in 1925, is considered as the largest organization that finances the multinational students exchange for researchers and teachers. DAAD also promotes postgraduate study programmes that enable students to complete their Masters and PhD. It is an association that constitutes of German higher education institutions and students from different cultures. Their main goal is to foster internationalization of German universities through enhancing and promoting the German language worldwide. For example, in Palestine, Birzeit University offers a Bachelor's degree in teaching Germany as a second language, a scheme that is in cooperation with the DAAD internationalization programme (DAAD, 2019).

In contrast with the aforementioned international scholarships, there is a local scholarship that is subsidized by the Bank of Palestine and is administered by a welfare foundation named Zamalah. The Zamalah Fellowship Program aims at ameliorating the quality of higher education and renovating the teaching methods in the Palestinian universities by coaching teachers academically, professionally and technically. The program trains academics at prominent international institutions for a duration ranging from two months to a whole year. This cooperation has sprouted from Palestine with the association of the Universiti Malaysia Sarawak (UNIMAS) to enable Master and PhD students to continue their studies by doing research. A total of 120 Palestinian academics have availed from this scholarship through various opportunities given by prominent universities around the world (Zamalah, 2018).

What makes this program unique is the fact that the whole funding is through Palestinian sources, yet the international role intervenes only in adopting the scholars to study in their universities. This is an example of intercultural communication and cooperation that is funded nationally while the academic support is done internationally.

In addition, in Palestine, the European Union enhances the capacity building of the higher education system through one of its programmes which is Erasmus+ established in 2014 after the initiation of Erasmus Mundus, Tempus and Jean Monnet. It consists of three components that are situated under key actions. First, International Credit Mobility (ICM) which is under Key action1 and is concerned with the mobility of individuals, whether they are students who leave their home universities to enroll in other international universities for a semester or two or university staff who work in the education sector both in teaching or training capacities. The second component is the Capacity Building in Higher Education (CBHE) that funds and builds mainly the capacity of universities and then other private sectors. Palestine has won 50 CBHE projects with around a 44-million- Euro budget and approximately 5 million Euros from 2007 till 2019 on mobilizing around 2200 students and staff mobility opportunities allocated for the Palestinians (National Erasmus Office in Palestine). The researcher amplifies in details about the aforementioned components in chapter two.

Among all the previously mentioned foreign aids, the researcher, in this paper, conducts a study on the impact of Erasmus+ higher education aid on enhancing intercultural communication in Palestine.

1.3. Statement of the Problem

There are a lot of programs that are subsidized by the United States, British Council, Germany and the European Union such as DAAD, Fulbright, USAID, Chevening and Hespal and much more.

These international higher education aids enhance the development of higher education system and according to the World Bank, such aids are "the powerful driver of development"

(World Bank, 2019). However, Erasmus+, under the European Union support, empowers the quality in higher education since it is the biggest mechanism in funding higher education institutions in Palestine and elsewhere. It has numerous projects at the levels of CBHE and ICM. Palestine, under Erasmus+ programme, won 50 CBHE projects with around 44-million Euro budget and approximately 5 million Euros from 2007-2019 on mobilizing around 2200 students and staff mobility opportunities allocated for the Palestinians. Most studies focus on the development of higher education whereas limited studies are conducted to assess the quality of higher education. However, there has not been any scholarly publication that studies its impact and its effectiveness in Palestine. Therefore, this study aims at studying the following aspects: The researcher intends to investigate if the Erasmus+ as a mechanism with its 44 million budget enhances or has a tangible effect on enhancing intercultural communication and cooperation through their funding projects among Palestine, the regional countries in Europe and the Middle East. Moreover, the researcher wants to inspect if Erasmus+ has strengthened the cooperation between Palestinians' and Europeans' higher education institutions. In addition, this study aims at examining whether Erasmus+ has been able to bridge the socio-cultural gap between Palestine and European countries and promote cultural knowledge between Palestine and Europe, and to see if Erasmus+ synergies yield any sustainable development. Finally, it examines the impact of the cultural interaction between the higher education institutions.

1.4. Aim and Objectives of the Study

1.4.1. Aim:

The study aims at investigating the impact of Erasmus+ higher education aid on enhancing intercultural communication in Palestine.

1.4.2. Objectives:

More specifically, the study has the following objectives:

- To investigate whether Erasmus+ genuinely helps in cooperation and intercultural communication between Palestinians and Europeans.
- To see if Erasmus+ bridges the socio-cultural gaps between the higher education system in the Palestinian and the European institutions.
- To assess if Erasmus+ projects contribute in promoting the cultural knowledge between Palestine and Europe.
- To see if these projects yield sustainable cooperation.
- To examine the impact of the cultural interaction between the higher education institutions on both the Palestinians and Europeans.

1.5. Questions of the Study

The study aims at answering the following questions:

1.5.1 The Main Question of the Study

What is the impact of Erasmus+ higher education aid on enhancing intercultural communication in Palestine?

1.5.2 The Sub-Questions of the Study:

- To what extent does the Erasmus+ genuinely help in cooperation and intercultural communication between the Palestinians and the Europeans higher education institutions?

- Does Erasmus+ bridge the socio-cultural gaps between the higher education system in the Palestinian and the European institutions? If yes, in what ways?

• Do Erasmus+ projects contribute in promoting the cultural knowledge between Palestine and Europe? If yes, how?

• To what extent do these projects yield sustainable cooperation?

What is the impact of cultural interaction between the higher education institutions at the national, institutional, individual level?

1.7. The Significance of the Study

Most related literature is oriented towards evaluating the outputs and outcomes of Erasmus+ projects. However, there is no study, as far as the researcher knows, sought in the impact of enhancing intercultural communication and cooperation between Palestine and the regional countries in Europe and the middle East. One important goal in the initiation of Erasmus+ programme is to strengthen cooperation and intercultural communication nationally, regionally and internationally among the constituents of the higher education system. Therefore, this current study investigates the impact of Erasmus+ 50 CBHE projects and around 2200 ICM mobilities, on enhancing intercultural communication between Palestine, Europe and the Arab world through applying the qualitative analysis approach on a sample taken from most Palestinian universities that constitute 80% of the population of the study. This study is unique because it is the only scholarly publication in this area. The researcher will review the literature in this area in more depth in the region. Moreover, the results of the study will help the Ministry of Palestinian of Higher Education to better enhance cooperation with other regional and international higher education institutions. This cross-cultural cooperation is estimated to internationalize the higher education system whether through the ICM exchange mobilities or the multinational CBHE projects cooperation. It will promote diversity, social interaction and integration among students, staff, professors and the higher education system in Palestine and worldwide.

1.8. Limitations of the Study

- Place/Location: the study is limited within Erasmus+ Palestine and its Programme.

- Time: the study has been conducted in the year 2020. Moreover, the targeted CBHE projects have been limited to the years 2015-2019.

- Objective: to investigate the impact of Erasmus+ higher education aid on enhancing intercultural communication.

- Sample: the researcher checks out the impact of Erasmus+ projects through collecting data from most of the Palestinian universities. The population is the sum of the CBHE projects and the ICM. In Palestine, there are 50 CBHE projects with 44 million euro and around 2200 ICM mobilities. The sample includes most of the population from the Palestinian universities impacted by the programme and which constitutes 80% of the population of the study.

1.9 Summary

The chapter tackles the significance of the international higher education in the world and in Palestine. It shows how Palestine depend on the international aid due to their infrastructure destruction that is caused by the war and occupations. Thereafter, it sheds the light on Erasmus+ European funding that is the core of this case study. Moreover, the rest of the chapter is divided into the statement of the problem, the aim and objectives of the study, the questions of the study, and finally the limitations of the study. The next chapter discusses the operational definitions that are used in this thesis and the theoretical background of Erasmus commencement history that leads afterwards to the formation of Erasmus+. Moreover, the next chapter also tackles the ICM and CBHE studies that are conducted in order to compare and contrast these studies with the researcher current study.

Chapter two

Theoretical Background

Review of the Related Literature

Chapter Two
Theoretical Background
Review of the Related Literature

2.1. Preview

This chapter addresses the theoretical frame work and the historical background of Erasmus+ program. It tracks the stages of the European programs funding that ranges from 2007-2020 and ending with the establishment of Erasmus+ with all the mobilities and projects funded by the European Union committee and implemented by Erasmus+ worldwide programs. Moreover, it also displays its effect globally. In order to highlight Erasmus+ activities, the researcher presents his/her work by mentioning the Key Actions of Erasmus+, the international credit mobility (ICM), and the capacity building of higher education (CHBE). Moreover, the researcher expatiates her demonstration on ICM and CBHE to detect their impact on different cultures and precisely the Palestinian culture. This vividly appears in the chosen related literature conducted by various scholars.

2.2. Theoretical Background

2.2.1Operational Definitions

- **European Union**:

It is the donor that funds such enormous programme as Erasmus+ with 16.5 billion Euro to facilitate the implementation of its projects in Southern Mediterranean Region, the Arab world and Palestine represented by the National Erasmus Office in particular since it is the case study that the researcher has conducted the study upon.

- **National Erasmus Office in Palestine**:

It is the representative office of the European Union that implements its programmes and activities. It acts as a mediator between the European Union and Higher Education System. See more details about National Erasmus Office in Palestine in section 2.2.10.

- **International Credit Mobility (ICM):**

It is one of Erasmus+ components that is called key action 1. It is consisted of 2200 incoming and outgoing student mobility from Palestine to Europe or vice versa with a budget of 5 million euros. It resembles the population of the researcher case study that the sample is taken from to build the research upon. Moreover, through this student exchange mobility the researcher investigates the impact of this component that is one of Erasmus+ components on most of Palestinians universities, in order to measure the degree of intercultural communication, cooperation, integration, social interaction and internationalization among the Palestinian higher education institutions with the outgoing or incoming students and staff that either studies or train for a certain period of time and other international higher education institutions.

- **Capacity Building of Higher Education (CBHE):**

It is one of Erasmus+ components that is called key action 2. It is mainly responsible for building the capacity of higher education institutions such as universities, colleges, vocational institutions and other private sectors by modernizing and internationalizing the quality of higher education and renovating the curricula with other European universities. This cooperation aims at bridging the gap between what is taught in academia and what the labor market really needs. It consists of 50 projects, including ongoing projects, that Erasmus+ national Palestine won with a budget of 44 million euros. Moreover, it resembles the population of the researcher case study that the sample is taken from to build the research upon. In addition, through CBHE projects the researcher investigates the impact of this component that is one of Erasmus+ components on most of Palestinians universities, in order to see if these projects led to have strong intercultural relations, integration and communication among Palestinian higher education and its international counterpart. The researcher conducts her study on the sample that constitutes 80% of the sum of Erasmus+ CBHE and ICM projects taken from most of Palestinians universities.

- **Ongoing Projects:**

These are Erasmus+ CBHE projects that begins at a certain period of time and their impact is not measured yet since it is still on process of completion. The duration lasts three years before reaping its returns.

- **International Higher Education:**

Through Erasmus+ ICM mobilities and CBHE projects the Palestinian higher education is internationalized. That is by the mutual synergies that are undergone between Palestinian higher education institutions and Europeans. This internationalization is mainly focused on the modernization of Palestinian higher education and is implemented by sending students and staff abroad to learn new techniques and programs that help them to think critically and can implement it in their home universities. Moreover, the mutual CBHE projects seek to ameliorate the whole educational system through renovating its curricula and upgrading the capacity of its professors by sending them abroad to other international universities in order to be trained with new techniques to elevate Palestinian higher education cadre.

- **International Aid:**

Palestine went under occupation and still is which led to the deconstruction of the economic and educational infrastructure. Therefore, Palestine needed international fund to lift them from poverty, and upgrade and elevate their education level. There are numerous international funding programs the United States, British council, Chevening and much more. Erasmus+ is one of the programs that European Union funds and is the core of the researcher study case.

- **Case Study:**

It is the study that the researcher engages, using Palestine as a focal country, while describing the impact of Erasmus+ projects on the Palestinian higher education institutions. In this study, the researcher measures and describes the impact at three levels. The individual level, the institutional level and the national level.

- **Intercultural Communication**:

The researcher manifests intercultural communication throughout the thesis by shedding the light on Erasmus+ programme. Moreover, the researcher demonstrates the role of Erasmus+ in bridging the socio-cultural gaps by enhancing cross-cultural communication through learning languages and some behavioral norms, thus; adjacent cultural thinking and eliminate barriers that occur among people.

A successful project begins with firm internal communications then expand to have external communications with European universities. The study illustrates throughout the thesis the role of each stakeholder, staff and student in strengthening the relationships between each other and between them and international universities.

Furthermore, Erasmus+ projects in Palestine are explicitly visible examples on how these projects through cooperation and communication elevated the higher education level in Palestine, and helped in bridging the gap between academia and the labor market needs by introducing expertise to integrate in academia and improve student's competencies. The integration and communication has been occurred nationally, regionally and internationally. Wherefore, Erasmus+, through its projects, plays a crucial role in cultural convergence, cooperation and commerce. Some examples of Erasmus+ CBHE projects are PENs, uniGOV, TAP, METHODS and much more. These projects are amplified in details in the fourth chapter and also in the appendices.

- **Cultural Identity:**

It is one of the socio- cultural gaps that Erasmus+ bridges through its projects. In this research it is clearly shown in the local study of the related review studies that Erasmus+ has been able to bridge the cultural identity of a Palestinian – Israeli student that has come from a closed family with societal and religious obligations. Moreover, it also shows how studying abroad did not affect her identity. On the contrary, Erasmus+ has played a major role in transforming and reshaping the girl's cultural identity and that is by deconstructing her norms to fit within other cultures which made her express herself easily.

Wherefore, it has been shown that Erasmus+ promotes equity among its participants and urge for cultural emergence and convergence throughout it implemented projects.

2.2.2. The History of Erasmus+

The European Union supports its member states to provide elite education and training programs for its citizens and likewise other correlated countries. Through its encouragement of the exchanging student mobility, it improves the quality and efficiency of education and training. Moreover, it promotes equity among its people. (Education, Training and Youth, 2019). It also plays a tremendous role in human development, mainly in strengthening the international relations through empowering education worldwide, that is by building the capacity of the Higher Education system and elevating the educational level worldwide. These effective synergies have increased the global relations through funding enormous programmes. One of the programs that it launches is the Erasmus+ program. It dates back to 2014 and consists of many components.

Before the initiation of the Erasmus+ programme, there were different programmes funded by the European Union to support and modernize the higher education system in Europe and in the world. Some of these programs used to be called Erasmus Mundus, Jean Monnet and Erasmus Tempus. Erasmus Mundus is an international, cooperative and mobility program in the field of higher education that consolidates the quality of European higher education through a joint master and doctorate degree scholarship by fostering cooperation between the European Union and different cultures in the third countries. It aims at internationalizing the higher education human capital which are students and staff and also develop international collaborative projects and research (Mertefa, 2019). However, Tempus program supported the modernization of higher education in partner countries in Eastern Europe, central Asia, the Western Balkans and the Mediterranean region pre-eminently through university cooperation projects and exchanging educational experience (Mertefa, 2018). Jean Monnet, on the other hand, is an educational project funded by the European Union and aims at supporting the academic teaching and research in the field of European studies. It fosters the European integration through dialogue between academics and policy makers on the one hand, and people and cultures on the other hand. The anticipated outcome of this programme is measured through the impact on young graduates. Jean Monnet programme support researchers who had acquire PhD and maximize staff chances to promote their careers. Moreover, all higher education institutions throughout the world whether active organizations in the European union subject or researchers specializing in European union studies (Anonymous, 2019).

Thereafter, precisely in 2014, Erasmus+ has emerged, and its programs are still rolling up to 2020. This program, although replacing Erasmus Tempus and Mundus, still has the same function. The European Union has allocated a budget of 16 and a half billion euros to fund the different components of Erasmus+ for the entire world (European Commission, 2015). The first component of Erasmus+ is key action 2 CBHE which is the capacity building of higher education that funds and builds the capacity of universities mainly and other private sectors. The other component is ICM which is international credit mobility. This component used to be called Erasmus mundus, a program that used to have scholarships for full master degree and PhD. More precisely, the ICM is an exchange student mobility that mainly helps the mobility of students to study a semester or two in Europe or Palestine. All of these components constitute what is called Erasmus+.

These key actions are beneficial for Palestine. There are 50 CBHE projects with around a 44-million-euro budget and approximately 5 million euros from 2007 till 2019 on mobilizing around 2200 student and staff mobility opportunities allocated for the Palestinians (National Erasmus Office in Palestine). This enormous budget is used to develop ongoing projects that Erasmus+ offers to individuals and organizations depending on which programme or partner country they belong to. The researcher addresses the role of Erasmus+ broadly and pays tribute to the European Union manifestation. Moreover, the researcher particularizes National Erasmus Office in Palestine as the main study in this research. It is worth mentioning that Erasmus+ functions through an agency called EACEA, Education, Audiovisual and Culture Executive Agency that is located in Brussels, Belgium and runs part of the union programs. It is also concerned with Erasmus+ actions. Moreover, the European Union commission is accountable for Erasmus+ policies and presides the overall implementation process. Since the researcher demonstrates the components of Erasmus+, she focalizes on the role of Erasmus+ toward the international credit mobility considering that it is the main issue the researcher is dealing with in her research. Other components are also mentioned but not in profound description. Therefore, the researcher gives much focus to Erasmus+ main key actions which are the (ICM- Key Action 1), (CBHE- Key Action 2).

2.2.3. The International Credit Mobility (ICM)

The International Credit Mobility is mainly concerned about individuals. Therefore, it is one of the motifs that Erasmus+ consists of and is considered the main pillar to mobility. Moreover, it is the exchange student and staff mobility that enables students to practice a semester or two in Europe or other country whether countries stated under programme or partner countries. Likewise, staff mobility is concerned with those working in education both in teaching and training capacities. Staff are invited to teach at a partner higher education institution from five days to two months. A partner country staff mobility can also train at a non-academic programme country. Moreover, staff can also bind their training period with teaching aiming at helping students to interact culturally and acquire specific skills which enable them to brace and evolve their understanding of other cultures (CSUDAY, 2019). ICM grant rates differ from programme countries to partner countries. Since the researcher focal study is Palestine which is situated in the Southern Mediterranean Region, the monthly rate for ICM is 700 Euro per student; whereas, staff daily rate is 180 Euro (CSUDAY, 2019). The closest the participant's destination to the place of study or train, the cheaper it would be. So, as for partner countries which travel a distance of 8000km or more, the amount of travel allowance is 1500 Euro per participant.

2.2.4. Participation in ICM

In order for a partner country like Palestine to participate, any institution must be recognized as a higher education institution and therefore sign an inter- institutional agreement with their programme country before proceeding the mobility process. In other words, if the institution is not a higher education one, the agreement is ineligible and must be recuperated. On the other hand, other organizations from both programme and partner countries can join the ICM mobilities. However, these organizations should be related to labor markets or the field of education, training and youth. Also, these organizations can host students from traineeship or staff for training. Thus, it is a mutual process where both can benefit equally (CSUDAY, 2019).

2.2.5. Roles and Responsibilities

The organization, in charge of the application process, sends the applications on behalf of their partners to the national agency. Upon selecting the successful applications, the beneficiary organization, which is always the programme country higher education institution, signs the grant agreement and arranges it. Finally, it gives a report about its consequences. The partner countries' organizations are responsible for nominating the students and staff for the grant and sending them abroad. Furthermore, they prepare them for what they actually face during their studies or training period. At last, students are welcomed from either a programme country or a partner country who provide them with support during their stay (CSUDAY, 2019).

2.2.6. Timeline for ICM Proposal

Projects for proposals are based annually on a proposal call by the European commission every October to be started in August of the same year. The selection is maneuvered by national agencies in the case of programme countries; whereas, in the case of partner countries, Erasmus+ offices are the ones who are in charge. The grant application must be submitted ultimately by 12:00 noon Brussels time. The ICM projects or what is called KA107 runs from two years to three calendar years. The beginning and the end of the projects must fit within the time scale. The budget allocation of the ICM is shown below the following figure that Cunningham highlights in one of his slides presentation "International Credit Mobility"

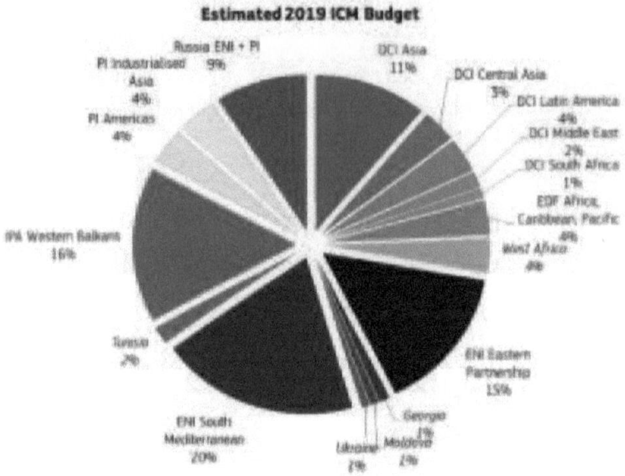

Figure 1 Estimated International credit mobility budget pie chart 2019. Adapted from "Erasmus+ international credit mobility," by P. Cunningham, 2019, Slideplayer.com. Retrieved December 25, 2019

This figure shows a graph that consists of twelve discrete envelopes covering each region of the world. The largest share is allocated to the Southern Mediterranean Region which is stated under partner countries with 21% budget. 2% is for the Middle East including Palestine whereas other remaining budget is distributed respectively between other partner and programme countries. National agencies are required to fund projects with partner countries that are of low income and less developed (Cunningham, 2019).

2.2.7. Countries Covered in Erasmus+ Projects:

Programme countries involved in Erasmus+ are the member states of the European Union which are: Belgium, Bulgaria, Czech Republic, Denmark, Germany, Estonia, Ireland, Greece, Spain, France, Croatia, Italy, Cyprus, Latvia, Lithuania, Luxembourg, Hungary, Malta, Netherlands, Austria, Poland, Portugal, Romania, Slovenia, Slovakia, Finland, Sweden, United Kingdom. However, non-European programme countries are: Former Yugoslavs, Republic of Macedonia, Turkey, Norway,

Iceland, Liechtenstein. Moreover, Erasmus+ funds participating countries which are divided into two groups: Western Balkans: Albania, Bosnia, Herzegovina, Kosovo, Montenegro and also Eastern Partnership countries which are: Armenia, Azerbaijan, Belarus, Georgia, Moldova, territory of Ukraine. On the other hand, South-Mediterranean countries such as Algeria, Egypt, Israel, Palestine, Jordan, Lebanon, Libya, Morocco, Syria, Tunisia, Russia also have the biggest share of funding (Participating, 2019).

2.2.8. The ICM Application Process

According to CSUDAY (2019), the programme country higher education institutions fill the application form and send it to their national agency to facilitate the process of finding a partner institution. The programme country higher education institutions must have a clear description of their programmes and their teaching assessment and must be accepted by the partners' institutions. If the institution is reluctant about mutual agreements, it can begin with staff mobility to ensure confidence before involving students in this partnership. Program countries must have an Erasmus charter for higher education (ECHE). It is an indispensable framework for programme countries which is taken within Erasmus+ in order to participate in learning mobility of individuals or through cooperation for innovation. In contrast, partner countries are not required to obtain (ECHE) and their quality framework is established through inter-institutional agreements between higher education institutions. Both the programme and the partner countries need a participant identification code (PIC) that identifies every organization involved in ICM. Without the PIC, academic organizations cannot take part in this mobility unless they are registered through the European Commission to have one. Whereas, non-academic organizations for traineeship or staff mobility do not need a PIC.

As for the application form, the programme country institution can only apply for one application per call yet have a limitless number of partner countries and that is in order to avoid double funding. If an institution is applying solely, the programme country must have the Erasmus charter of higher education (ECHE) and the participant identification code (PIC) linked to the Erasmus code. National agencies have the right to sift which partner project is likely to be funded and which is not or to reduce mobilities or not due to the European Union limited budget. The applicants are supposed to anticipate the outcome of the project, its relevance, what qualities they may gain out of it, and what impact it drops on each partner country. Once the ICM project is selected for fund, the programme country institution signs an agreement linked with their national agency. The ICM projects with partner countries are listed and evaluated by experts who are assigned by Erasmus+.

Before any mobility activity, there is an inter-institutional agreement which is a mutual procedure undertaken between the programme institution and their partner countries and this agreement includes all the mobility activities before implementation. Only rectors of these institutions are eligible to sign the agreement. Afterwards, students sign the learning agreement which should have all the learning outcomes the students gain during their period of study abroad. Furthermore, they are selected upon certain criteria with an academic merit but preferably those with socio-economic less advantaged backgrounds. Students are allowed to enroll several times up to 12 months per study cycle. Once they are selected, they receive a study chart that explains their rights and obligations while studying abroad. The selectees are given a mobile tool^{+} so that the programme country institution inserts the participants' monthly and final update report in order for the European Commission to monitor their progress easily. In addition to their previous duties, national agencies in programme countries are responsible for monitoring how the ICM project is proceeding and sharing their support with the beneficiary organizations and also gather information on project implementation. However, in partner countries, National Erasmus Offices are the ones who are responsible for managing the ICM project with the international higher education institutions in 27 partner countries. They are eligible to monitor all ICM projects and ensure their implementation. For traineeship, non-academic organizations in both programme and partner countries are eligible to host students or traineeship who are active either in labor market or in the fields of education, training and youth with a public or a private enterprise, nonprofit organizations and vocational education.

To epitomize what the ICM application process is, the researcher gives a quick view on the process in order to make it easier for the reader to understand. The European commission has a delegation agreement with the programme higher institutional agency. This national agency is responsible for the assessment of the national application form that is issued on February and also for the grant agreement. An institutional agreement is held between the programme and the partner higher education institutions and that is before the commencement of the practical mobility which takes place on the first of August. The project duration is from 24 to 36 months. An assessment of the mobility is required once every month. Therefore, a monthly report is added in the mobility tool^{+}. Two reports are required to be submitted to the national agency. One is an interim report and another one is a final beneficiary report to track the progress of mobility. A tripartite agreement is held between the programme higher education institution, the partner country higher education institution and the participants. This takes place before the start of the actual mobility. Before encoding mobilities in mobility tool^{+}, participants must have a PIC. Staff participants are required to fill out an online survey report after their five weeks training period. Nevertheless, students are required to fill out a recognition survey to assess the quality of recognition.

2.2.9. ICM and the Cultural Aspect

Taking National Erasmus Office in Palestine as a Special Case

The researcher depicts, in her research, the enrollment of some students and their attribute in the mobility exchange programme Erasmus+ both the outgoing and incoming students within Europe and also the exchange from Europe to Palestine and vice versa. These students and staff demonstrate their role in this exchange and how it has benefited them culturally. A European study done by the CHE [1]consult group (Souto-Otero, 2019) tracks the European ICM students between the years 2017-2019 in order to assess the impact of ICM on students and their culture. The study finds out that students who complete an Erasmus+ mobility for studying or training boost their employability skills; they become creative in solving problems and communicate better with others. According to European statistics, 72% of those students are immediately employed. Moreover, it increases their technical and inter-personal skills and maintains social cohesion. Their intercultural competency progresses since individuals interact with others from different cultures. They develop a tendency towards accepting others and that is obvious in their strong self- confidence and autonomy. The longer they stay abroad, the more outright their foreign language becomes and that is through communicating with their foreign colleagues. Their competencies are built through collaborative working, resilience and embracing new techniques that enable them to enhance their studies in their home

---

[1] CHE consultant of higher education Management.

countries. Furthermore, 40% of students who attend a traineeship are offered jobs by their host country during their training period. Some also establish their own businesses while others have a clear vision of their future career. The mobility lets students experience new methods which positively increase their motivation and improve their competences. It motivates them to proceed to a higher level of studies. As for Europeans, they become loyal to Europe and strengthen their identity by interacting with citizens.

Furthermore, ICM students in Palestine have their whack to explore European countries. National Erasmus Office in Palestine gives students opportunities to benefit from the grants by sending them abroad to participate in the exchange student mobility. The researcher shares ICM stories of some students whose actual participation is reflected on their personal traits and social cohesiveness. Ahmad Albuhais, a Gazan citizen who had the opportunity to join Erasmus+ mobility, for him, this opportunity has opened his mind to new horizons (National Erasmus Office in Palestine, 2019). He has got a scholarship for Master's degree to the university of Oldenburg in Germany after finishing his Bachelor's in computer engineering at the Islamic University in Gaza. He says:

> This so far was the best experience I had in my life. It changed me to the better; personally, and professionally. I learned many new things, got the opportunity to use very new advanced technologies, worked on real projects for well-known companies, and became a very qualified big data engineer.

Ahmad has also learned to speak German and met people from different cultures.

Another example that illustrates the ICM reciprocation is the incoming mobility to Palestine. Riccardo Corradin, an Italian student who has had the chance to join Erasmus+ exchange programme, comes from the university of Siena in Italy majoring in emergency surgery. He has enrolled in the Islamic university in Gaza. According to him, he reports that he has captured new techniques in surgery that he thinks have added to his knowledge. He has felt intimate with the Gazan people and felt at home. Moreover, Riccardo adds that his experience in Gaza was due to the huge casualties he encountered during the war which far exceed the casualties in Italy. Riccardo transfers this experience to his colleagues in Italy to benefit from what he learned in his Erasmus+ mobility (Ruptly, 2019).

Nargiz Mammadova is another incoming student mobility to Palestine from Azerbaijan and Master's student at Siena University in Italy. She came to Palestine on the 30th of January, 2019 and enrolled in the cultural diplomacy program. Mammadova says that Erasmus+ was a turning point in her life that contributed to expand her vision of the world. During her 3 months-stay at Birzeit University, she perceived people's hospitality and was fascinated by the Palestinian's rich cuisine. Moreover, her part-time job has helped her integrate with the Palestinian culture. This opportunity has helped shape her character as a person. Her stay in Palestine has also strengthened her inter-personal traits and built up her self-confidence and autonomy (Birzeit University, 2019).

Not only does Erasmus+ present a promising future for a specific category of students, but it also gives equal opportunities to disability ones. Fatma Lulu, a Gazan student in the Islamic University of Gaza, studied English literature and got accepted in the University of Glasgow in the UK for three months. Fatma says that this opportunity was a turning point in her life, too. Her skills have been developed and she has been exposed to methods of teaching which helped her improve her domain of studies. Consequently, she has become self- confident and got the chance to present herself and speak in front of Scottish people, the thing that enhanced her self- autonomy. Moreover,

Fatma's disability did not prevent her from getting along with others. On the contrary, she built strong relationships and made close friends. Glasgow's people were intimate, social and loyal, Fatma concludes (Erasmus+ Programme, 2019).

Similarly, staff mobility has its positive impact on universities, organizations, and culture as well. This opportunity allows the staff to improve their skills and competences. They learn new teaching techniques and research methods to transfer and implement in their own universities back home. Alongside with their personal and social development, they become interculturally competent. The mutual cooperation between universities that share common interest under Erasmus+ supports the curriculum and pedagogical development. This cooperation leads to the internationalization of teaching which, in return, enhances the quality of teaching and learning. In general, the impact of Erasmus+ on higher education not only enhances personal development but also helps in the ramification of correlations that reinforce international collaborative research projects. Moreover, according to Erasmus+ (2018), 44% of the staff used innovative methods while they were training abroad. This training was the cause for their promotion in their institutions. Staff from different institutions were invited to teach and exchange experiences to elevate students' knowledge and skills in order to accommodate with the labor market. In Palestine and through the National Erasmus office, students and staff from different universities located in different Palestinian cities are engaging in this mobility. The university sends their staff through Erasmus+ either to teach or to train. Those who teach get a chance to teach at an educational institution abroad. Staff from outside the educational sector are given the chance to share their experience and knowledge, too. On the other hand, some go for training that consists of job shadowing, observation periods or other training courses. For instance, Birzeit University is one of the well- known Palestinian universities that join student and staff mobility. On the third of October, 2019, Birzeit university has launched a staff for teaching and training mobility to NOVA University Lisbon in Portugal through Erasmus+. These mobilities help in bringing new methods and techniques that renovated the students' capabilities to become resilient with new technologies. Erasmus+ Palestine in this particular domain, aims at developing the teaching techniques and methods utilized at the Palestinian universities to convoy the rapid Western evolution and growth. In addition, An-Najah National University shares an equal role of sending staff outside their university under Erasmus+. In 2018, they sent staff to Naples to increase their academic knowledge in order to update the student's skills. These two universities (An-Najah and Naples) are just an example of what Erasmus+ provides. It also provides support to other Palestinian universities located in the West Bank and Gaza Strip such as: Palestinian Technical University, The Arab American University, Khadoorei University, The Islamic University in Gaza and many more (National Erasmus+ Office- Palestine, 2019, p. 3).

2.2.10. The Capacity Building of Higher Education (CBHE) and its Impact on Culture

Key action 2 the Capacity Building in Higher Education (CBHE) is one of Erasmus+ programmes. The main aim of CBHE is to modernize and internationalize the quality of higher education. It also fosters the networking and cooperation between the European and the Partner Countries. In other words, it is mainly concerned with the renovation and amendments of the higher education through modernizing and institutionalizing its programs in partner countries. Therefore, it is a mutual cooperation that conjoins both the eligible partner countries with the European Union. Furthermore, CBHE consists of multinational versatile projects foremost between programme higher education institutions and eligible partner countries. These projects reinforce partner countries and promote vis a vis communication among people to integrate different cultures and bring intercultural awareness as well as clear grasp among them. Challenges and barriers are multilaterally addressed and resolved. Organizations from eligible partner countries, chiefly higher education institutions, cooperate with programme countries to ameliorate and upgrade the quality of higher education in order to bridge the gap between what is taught in academia and the labor market preference. Through this cooperation, new education programmes are implemented that elevate higher education skills. The renovation does not only focus on strengthening the capacity of management, internationalization and innovation of institutions, but also aims at promoting the capacity of the national HEIs in order for them to modernize their own higher education systems. Contemporizing is done through adapting new methods and techniques from different regions of the world. There are two types of projects within the CBHE: structural projects and joint projects. The joint projects aim at supporting organizations from partner countries through modernizing and developing the curriculum whereas structural projects intend to innervate and redress the higher education system through rectifying its policies both on national or regional level.

Organizations that tend to apply for CBHE proposals must be either a higher education institution or any organization of the higher education institution and mainly from the participant eligible partner countries. Calls announcement are notified annually through the national agencies of the European Union and under EACEA's supervision. Higher education institutions from partner countries participate in the proposal calls. Any project winners are considered grant holders and other organizations participating with them are partners. The duration of projects lasts from two to three years and the grants vary from 500,000 to one million euro, and this budget is used to cover travel expenses, equipment, and other activities.

Palestine has won 50 projects disseminated through various Palestinian universities since 2007. These projects have led to the rejuvenation of the Palestinian curricula and that is by incubating new courses and methodologies through joint programmes with other international higher education institutions. Moreover, the level of competences and skills of the Palestinian universities are improving to suit the labor market needs. It enhances joint researches and development. Not only does this renovation confine to Palestinian curricula, but it also contributes to the improvement of higher institutions and academic staff. (European Union, 2019)

2.2.11. National Erasmus in Palestine

Erasmus+, represented by National Erasmus Office in Palestine, is one of the European programmes that supports projects, partnerships and mobilities among students and staff in Palestine. It targets areas of education, training, youth and sports. Palestine has won 50 CBHE projects and 5 million ICM since 2007 that are implemented at the Palestinian universities with the cooperation of regional universities, European universities and the private sectors with a budget of 44 million Euros. Around 2200 Palestinian students have benefited from this exchange mobility by leaving Palestine to study a semester or two in a European country. Likewise, 325 European students are given the chance to study in Palestinian Universities for a semester or two. The European students face lots of occupational barriers while trying to reach the Palestinian territories preventing them to enroll in Palestinian universities at the specific registration time. This cooperation with the European countries also includes staff mobility. Palestinian staff are sent to European higher educational institutions and other organizations in order to gain experience to renovate the Palestinian curricula.

Likely, staff from Europe come to Palestine to train university students to implement new methods and procedures and to convoy the European innovation and technologies. This integration enhances the globalization of education in Palestinian universities. Moreover, Erasmus+ supports Palestinian universities financially, economically and academically through quality interventions. It develops new international programs that Palestinian universities lack such as Master's on software engineering, electronic engineering and e- government. Furthermore, it also modernizes teaching methods and that is through the inclusion of new strategic techniques. The European- Palestinian synergies lead to the renovation of the Palestinian higher education system in order to bridge the gap between education and the labor market. The renovation of the curricula is also implemented by bringing expertise to elevate Palestinian professors to adapt perfectly to the needs of the job market. National Erasmus Office in Palestine has won 7 projects with a budget of 5 million euros that aim at modifying the Palestinian higher education outputs to suffice the needs of the labor market. The modernization of the Palestinian curricula is done through the higher education reform experts (HEREs). They play a major role in forming the higher education policy. These experts are policy makers and academics who work with the ministry of higher education and Scientific Research and they come from different backgrounds. Their main concern is higher education polices and how to blend e-learning and entrepreneurship with education.

Finally, Erasmus+ has the most projects of the Southern Mediterranean region and Northern Africa. It has won 19 projects as grant holder. The European Union's budget allocation will geminate from the year 2021 to 2026 with a 30 billion euro (National Erasmus Office in Palestine, 2019).

2.3. Review of Related Studies

Erasmus+ programme is an international programme that is located worldwide. The researcher intends to review some related literature done on this programme in Europe and the Southern Mediterranean Region if applicable. The related literature is mixed literature concerning both the international credit mobility and the capacity building of higher education. ICM literature is concerned with the individual mobility while CBHE is concerned with the projects done to ameliorate the capacity building of the higher education institutions. Both the ICM and the CBHE are classified into foreign, Arab and local studies. The researcher has found four foreign ICM studies and one local study. However, four CBHE studies and reports have been found. Through these related literature, the researcher points out where these studies intersect with the researcher study and how the later differs from the provided literature making this study a unique one.

2.3.1. Foreign Studies (ICM, CBHE)

Due to globalization and the rapidly changing world, Erasmus+, through the European Union's endeavors, seeks to harmonize and upgrade the higher education systems by assuring internationalization and ensuring the quality of education in order to bridge the gap between academia and the labor market needs. By doing so, it tackles youth unemployment and tries to eliminate this dilemma. The first step to elevate youth academically and minimize their possibility of being unemployed is through enrolling them in the international credit mobility mechanism which serves as one of Erasmus+ pillars (VERHOEVEN, 2019). Below follows some literature review concerning student mobility (ICM).

Ricolfe & Pinto (2019) conducted a study on the motivation of Erasmus students to study abroad. The study's sample included 120 students from various engineering and other faculties in Universitat Politecnica in Spain. Personal interviews and survey method were the tools for this study. The study shows that Erasmus students from Western and Central Europe differ in their motivations to join Erasmus. Some were anticipating a future career through their academic studies while others were only just experiencing a new culture through their leisure moments. Students' behavior was measured through four factors: individual development, their choice of destination, their academic aspect, and their destination attraction. Moreover, the researchers recommended that university managers should take the psychological and social factors into consideration during their study period with Erasmus+. They should also offer them opportunities to help elevate their profession development by providing them with work and help their personal development by letting them practice their Spanish language outside class. Furthermore, universities should work with tourism sector in order to let students mingle in their culture. They also can help Erasmus students capture the Spanish language by organizing classes outside their schools.

As for Bryła, (2015), he piloted an empirical study to examine the impact of international student mobility on future career among Polish former Erasmus students. This study aimed at answering the research question which investigates whether international student mobility represented by Erasmus and other international student mobilities have a positive impact on the students' choice of career. The study used a questionnaire that was distributed among 14705 Polish alumni, including all Erasmus program participants in the year 2007-2008 (former students that joined Erasmus). After six years from studying abroad, the alumni were able to report in a survey conducted in

2012 their engagement in a career. The study shows that those alumni who participated in an international student mobility precisely Erasmus tend to have a fixed job with an international organization and their employers appreciate their work. They master a foreign language better than those students who did not participate in an international student mobility and had nonstable jobs. The study also revealed that Erasmus mobility contributes to multiple skills and competencies.

Moreover, (Jovanovska, Neshkovska, Trajkovska, Tabakovska, & Tasetovikj, 2018) escorted a study on the impact of student mobility on their academic achievements and their future ambitions. The aim of the study is to focus on the factors that hinder Macedonian students to exploit student mobility programs adequately. The results were obtained by distributing a quantitative survey among undergraduate and post-graduate students, in the university of St. Kliment Ohridiski, who are majored in administration and management in Macedonia. Two questionnaires were disseminated among a sample of fifty students out of 3000 in nearly ten period of time participating with student mobilities. The first questionnaire was about measuring the students' awareness of what benefits they can gain out of students' mobility, and the other questionnaire was about the reasons behind their ignorance of the benefits of student mobility abroad. The sample that was chosen were students who spent one semester at European universities within Erasmus+ programmes or CEEpus student mobility programme. Finally, the study shows that those participants who engaged in one of these student mobilities had their expectations met and they realized that they developed awareness of other cultures, and after the mobility they found themselves open to more acquaintances. They also gained inner trust and can function easily in their own country. Erasmus+ students became more aware of writing CVs and motivational letters, the thing that has boosted their chance to employability since employers view mobility as a positive experience. However, students who did not participate, reported that they would like to do so and recommend students mobility to others who had not got the chance to do so. Their non-participation was due to lack of information and trust and because they thought that the grants were previously distributed to specific students. Others complained that it was unclear and unhelpful and that they did not have any experience to apply to any job online due to their non-participation in student mobility. Moreover, the researchers recommend that student mobility information should be disseminated properly and should be informed of the multilateral benefits they are gaining from this mobility. Additionally, they prompt to enhance reliable information and establish contact with mobility coordinators. As well, they should organize events for graduates in order for them to share their previous experiences with students, and it must be on regular basis.

A similar study (Onen, 2017) investigates the impact of Erasmus+ mobility programme on the experience of Erasmus students. This study aims at examining the degree of Erasmus+ effectiveness on its participants and the reflection of such a programme on their academic, social, cultural, personal and career developments. It also aims at tracking the challenges they face (before, during, after) Erasmus+ period of mobility.

A survey with three parts was used to collect data: the first two parts were quantitative with a questionnaire distributed among 30 students and graduates who participated in the programme during 2010-2015 at Hayef Elt University. The data was collected from an online survey in order to encourage the participation of the graduates who used to be engaged in Erasmus+ mobility programme. However, the third part consists of open-ended questions that were accumulated through a qualitative approach.

The study finds out that, in spite of the bottlenecks the participants encountered in their mobility phase, they believed that their academic life and language acquisition were positively affected. To measure the difficulties that students faced, the researcher divided the students' mobility phase into periods. The most difficult period was the pre Erasmus+ period where students encountered a lot of obstacles during the paper work process. Moreover, students were unable to select their courses adequately, and they were not able to choose the courses equivalences. They also had problems with the learning agreement preparation and lacked communication with Erasmus+ coordinates both at home and host universities. Furthermore, during the Erasmus+ period students faced some problems while communicating and socializing among other students.

They also faced problems in using the language which was the German language since the German people lacked the capability of speaking English. In addition, students' major problem was the education system itself. There were differences in the requirements of the courses and the way the lessons were taught. The home university system was based on exams education whereas in the host university in Munich, Germany, it was based on presentations and project work.

Finally, some students faced the post- Erasmus+ syndrome since they found difficulty in adaptation to their university in the one hand and their adaptation to their city on the other hand. Some became shocked with the different educational system and lifestyle of Turkey (their own country) since they got accustomed to the relaxing and less trafficked country of Germany. The researcher of this study recommends that Erasmus+ coordinators and instructors encourage students to participate in Erasmus mobility, support them, and send as many students as possible. An orientation programme should be arranged before the departure of students in order for them to realize the possible

systems, and usage. The output of these tools are used to provide decision makers with tools that help them improve the quality of education inside the higher education system.

This ongoing project is assumed to have impacts on so many levels. As for the individual level, this project is to benefit both students and academic authorities. The later are to implement the project strategy and tools in order to help understand diverse educational process since it is a mutual academic project cooperation between Europe and Latin America. Students, on the other hand, are expected to encounter innovative curricula that upgrade their educational system and modernize their course of learning through the implementation of learning analytic project techniques.

Regarding the local, regional and institutional level, adopted tools are designed to improve the higher education decision-making process on the local level. Nevertheless, at the regional level, it is disseminated to share its experience using the learning analytics in Latin America's higher education system. Whilst at the institutional level, a methodology is to be formed to adopt tools that can help to improve the learning process in higher education on a bigger scale. Finally, Europeans can benefit from the output of the project by distributing it to new partners that can benefit from them on their upcoming projects.

Due to the perplexity of the academic contexts of higher education, Silva et al. (2018) conducted a study on the project of building the capacity of human resources of higher education to cope with curricula complexity in Southeast Asian countries. The project contains four consortiums, four institutions from Europe, and eight from Asia. It is led by the university of Dandang, Vietnam. Literature was analyzed to show the competencies staff need in order to develop their socio-economic skills, transversal skills, leadership, management and other skills needed in order to strengthen their capacity to perform well and cope with the internationalization of the curricula. This project is expected to have an impact on various levels. At the local and institutional level, the HR4ASIA project helps the Asian higher education institutions to renovate their human resources strategy by stating their needs and be able to confront any challenges they encounter during the internationalization training process. This gained European knowledge and experience are to be transformed to other higher education institutions in Asia. Moreover, at the regional level, the European- Asian project plan is disseminated, and the sustainability of the project is assured. Finally, at the individual level, the project aims at motivating the staff's interpersonal, transversal and technical skills. It also boosts their self- confidence enabling them to make decisions and solve any sudden obstacles during the project process. Moreover, staff are expected to be able to communicate and work with other members of the team project.

Erasmus+, in its enormous programme, seeks to equalize education and tackle disadvantaged and disable students. A study conducted by (Cinotti et al., 2018) to present the activities done by the MUSE European project has the aim to restore and strengthen the human capital in Latin America, Chile, Mexico and Argentina. The aim of the project is to improve learning conditions in higher education institutions for disabilities in order for them to have equal employment opportunities. Therefore, university of Bologna have trained 30 administrative and academic staff members from these partner countries and used an inclusive approach which includes pedagogical and ICT competences for disability students. This project is expected to have an impact on individuals such as administrative and staff of higher education institutions by building their capacity to deal with students of disabilities. As for institutions, it applies new pedagogical approach that renovates the curricula in order to suit students with special needs. The European cooperation is crucial to the extent that it facilitates the existence of students with disabilities in the higher education institutions.

2.3.3. Conclusion

Chapter two started with giving a historical background of Erasmus formation from 2007 that is used to be Erasmus Mundus, Tempus and Jean Monnet. Some is still having the same functions others change their function. This gradual transformation led to the formation of Erasmus+ in 2014 and still rolling up till now. The Erasmus+ programme is the European Union funding programme that is the researcher core study case. It is consisted of many components yet the researchers main focus is on the ICM mobilities and CBHE projects. The researcher amplifies in depth each component and terminate historical background with National Erasmus in Palestine accomplishments in both components. These accomplishments help the researcher to conduct the study by analyzing the impact of Erasmus+ mobilities and projects with the 44 million budgets on the Palestinian higher education. Thereafter, the researcher presents the literature review concerning both components.

By presenting some related studies concerning ICM and CBHE projects, the researcher compares and contrasts these studies with her intended study. The researcher has found five ICM studies, four of which are foreign studies ranging from qualitative to quantitative approach. These studies focus on the internal life of Erasmus+ students' mobility period and how these students engage in such mobility to get their utmost output and gain the maximum benefit in order to boost their employability. The fifth study is an Arab- local study which examines the impact of Erasmus+ on an Arab-Israeli female's cultural identity. These ICM studies have a different perspective from the researcher's study that is meant to investigate the impact of Erasmus+ projects on enhancing intercultural communication.

As for the CBHE studies, the researcher has also found four foreign studies and reports on projects using different methodologies. The study that is conducted by the project team of the European commission intersects with the researcher's study where both studies aim at showing the impact of these projects on promoting intercultural communication. In general, CBHE projects seek to internationalize the higher education system and empower human capital to be interculturally competent. All the aforementioned related studies focus on the outputs and outcomes of Erasmus+ projects whereas this current study investigates the impact of Erasmus+ 50 CBHE projects and 2200 ICM mobilities on enhancing intercultural communication between Palestine, Europe and the Arab world through applying the qualitative analysis approach on a sample taken from most Palestinian universities that constitute 80% of the population of the study. The researcher study tracks Erasmus+ projects from the onset and shows how these projects are built upon cooperation and intercultural communication among students, staff and stakeholders. This study focuses on the international relations beyond the intended projects. It is unique since it manifests in the intercultural communication among Palestinian universities and among other regional and international universities. What also makes it unprecedented is that it is the first publication in Palestine concerning the impact of higher education aid in intercultural communication.

Chapter Three

Methodology and Procedures

Chapter Three

Methodology and Procedures

3.1. Preview

The researcher in this chapter marks out the methods and approaches used to investigate the problem and answer the questions of the study to define the overall aim. The population and the sample of the study are also mentioned. Moreover, the researcher states the indicators that are used in collecting the data that will eventually be used in analyzing the data. Finally, a detailed description of the process is used in analyzing the data is included.

3.2. Methodology

The qualitative descriptive thematic relational content analysis is used in the collection and analysis of data to provide an in-depth and detailed interpretation of this research study. Moreover, the qualitative content analysis and the thematic analysis are stated under the qualitative descriptive content analysis. They are techniques used to analyze verbatim data and demystify the themes used in the study. Their main feature is a methodical process of categorizing and describing the facts used through the creation of themes (Vaismoradi et al., 2016).

The researcher uses the relational analysis to examine all the themes used in the study and to see their relationships with the factual data that is accumulated from the targeted universities. Moreover, the thematic descriptive content analysis is used to analyze these themes in order to answer the inquiries of the study (A. Tomberg & P. Tomberg, 2019)

Furthermore, the researcher uses the qualitative content analysis approach to describe the case study that is engaged. The researcher uses Palestine as an intended country to describe the impact of Erasmus+ projects on the Palestinian higher education institutions. The researcher measures and describes this impact at three levels. The individual level, the institutional level and the national level. Moreover, the researcher sorts and interprets in depth the documents gathered through the support of Erasmus office from various Palestinian universities. These documents are samples of Erasmus+ ICM mobilities and CBHE projects that the targeted universities participated in with the cooperation of the European Union Higher Education Institutions (HEIs). By using the qualitative approach, the researcher intends to mainly address the research question that aims at investigating the impact of Erasmus+ higher education aid on enhancing intercultural communication in Palestine. The qualitative analysis helps the researcher to describe the impact of Erasmus+ projects on the higher education institutions. Through describing the impacts of Erasmus+ projects, the researcher tracks the student and staff experiences and cooperation during their engagement with various projects. The researcher has held some interviews with the director of Erasmus+ programme and the coordinators of the targeted CBHE projects.

3.3. Tools of the Study

The researcher desk works all the gathered documents and templates that are related to Erasmus+ ICM mobilities and CBHE projects. Moreover, the researcher has conducted phone interviews with the director of Erasmus+ who has provided the researcher with feedback on these projects. Moreover, the researcher has also interviewed the coordinators of seven CBHE projects through a phone call. Those interviews have been recorded. Based on these documents, a representative sample of Erasmus+ projects that have impacts are reviewed and analyzed. The projects are: TEFL-ePAL, MS in Cyber Physical, TAP, METHODS, ROMOR, PENS and uniGOV. Moreover, a semi-structured phone interview has been mediated among the coordinators of these projects to allow interviewees to give in-depth responses and share their experiences in the project. The purpose of the interview is to answer standardized open-ended questions that reach the goal of the interview and answer the questions of the study. The interview consists of three specific questions. The researcher asked the coordinators of Erasmus+ targeted projects:

- To give a synopsis of their projects
- If the project is sustainable and if yes, how sustainability of the project is measured.
- To see if there are any unexpected outcomes and any new intercultural communication between Palestinian HEIs and the European Union.

A descriptive content analysis is used in describing the impact of Erasmus+ projects on various targeted Palestinian universities who participated in Erasmus+ projects. It is also used to quantify qualitative information by sorting and categorizing the selected data in order to compare them together to find similarities as well as differences between them. Moreover, it is convenient in answering the research questions in an appropriate and adequate way. The documents are coded or broken into categories that describe the impacts of Erasmus+ projects. The researcher uses the section of the impact in EACEA template form while accumulating the data from Palestinian universities to describe the impact of Erasmus+ projects at three levels: the individual level, the institutional level and the national level. The researcher defines the impact and sustainability in her research according to EACEA definition of these terms. Therefore, sustainability is defined by EACEA as the long-run benefits reaped after the termination of the project and Erasmus+ aid. Nevertheless, according to EACEA, impact is the reflection of the project effect on a bigger scale and wider environment and an interpretation of its changes whether positive, negative or neutral at different levels. A specific criterion is used in describing the impact of Erasmus+ projects which is adopted by EACEA. In describing the impact of Erasmus+ CBHE projects, the researcher uses the impact section in EACEA's Annex project monitoring template that the researcher obtains through Erasmus+ National Office in Palestine. This annex contains the indicators that the researcher uses as assessment criteria for evaluating the impact of Erasmus+ projects at three levels. The indicators which the researcher uses in evaluating Erasmus+ projects are the following:

1. **The Impact at the Individual Level**

- The rate of employability
- The vulnerable groups involvement including disadvantaged and special needs

2. **The Impact at the Institutional Level**

- The outcome of the projects beyond the projects' teams. (New courses, services, etc.)
- National cooperation activities between local universities on the one hand and the universities with the Ministry of Higher Education and Scientific Research on the other hand. (research projects and joint associations)

3. **The Impact at the National Level**

- Mutual cooperation between European and Palestinian institutions.

- Cooperation between higher education institutions and the stakeholders (NGOs and private sectors).

- Amelioration of lifelong learning approaches.

Erasmus+ ICM mobilities and CBHE projects must go through these indicators to ensure their sustainability. Moreover, to maintain projects results, there should be an adequate higher education institutional support and external support.

3.4. Population and Sample of the Study

The researcher uses the purposeful sampling to generate beneficial information through selecting and choosing Erasmus+ projects that have impacts and are conducted from 2015-2019 by various Palestinian Universities such as Birzeit University, Hebron University, An-Najah National University, University College of Applied Sciences, Islamic University of Gaza, Al Azhar university and Bethlehem University. The utmost goal of purposeful sampling is to acquire cases or documents that are saturated in information for the purpose of the study (Patton, 1990). This method of sampling is used because the researcher intentionally chooses which Erasmus+ projects to include in the study based on their ability to supply the thesis with beneficial data. The population of the study is the accumulation of Erasmus+ projects which are 50 CBHE projects and 2200 ICM mobilities with a budget of 44 million Euros. The researcher's sample of these 7 universities represent 41% of the Palestinian Universities whose impact can be described. The researcher chooses these seven universities because they are sufficient enough to supply the researcher with great volume of data to answer the research questions.

Moreover, in choosing these targeted universities, the researcher has taken into consideration their geographical distribution and the number of projects they have managed. The researcher has chosen some universities that are located in the West Bank and Gaza Strip. For example, the researcher has chosen Hebron University from the south and An-Najah National University from the North. Moreover, universities that have conducted multiple CBHE projects and won many projects either as partners or as grant holders like Birzeit University and An-Najah National University have been taken into consideration. The researcher selects from the projects what is beneficial in answering the research questions. Erasmus+ CBHE projects vary to include terminated projects whose effect is still running even after the ceased Erasmus+ funding, and few ongoing projects that its impact can be anticipated. A specific criterion is used in assessing the impact of Erasmus+ projects which is adopted by EACEA.

Erasmus+ has won 50 CBHE projects with a budget of 44 million euros from (2007- 2019). Moreover, there are 5 million euros for 150 ICM project from (2015-2019). Furthermore, Palestine, represented by the National Erasmus Office, has been granted to be project coordinators for 19 projects. In an interview, the director of Erasmus+ says: "We are the highest in the Southern Mediterranean region; we are coordinators for 19 projects". The following graph shows the number of projects that Palestine won as a grant holder.

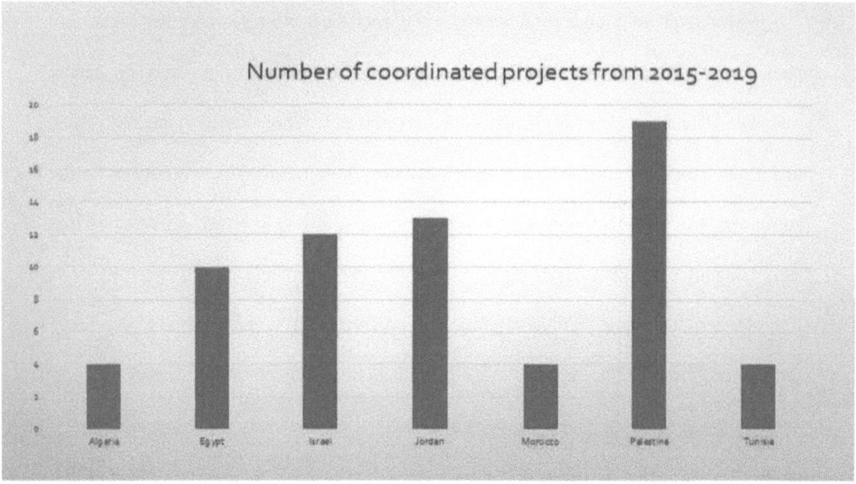

Figure 2 Number of Coordinated Projects from 2015- 2019. Adapted from National Erasmus Office in Palestine

3.5. Procedures of Analysis

The researcher has collected the documents, through Erasmus+ Office, from these specific universities who have participated in Erasmus+ ICM and CBHE projects and proved to have impact. The researcher, then, analyzes the data that describes the impact of every single university. The aim of this analysis is to investigate the impact of Erasmus+ higher education aid on enhancing intercultural communication in Palestine. This impact is measured according to EACEA's template form. The researcher uses the impact section from EACEA's field monitoring report that Erasmus+ National Office in Palestine has provided the researcher with. This section contains the indicators that the researcher uses as an instrument to gather the documents from these targeted Palestinian universities. After gathering the documents, the researcher categorizes them according to EACEA's indicators which assess Erasmus+ ICM and CBHE projects at three levels: the impact at individual level, the institutional level and the national level. The researcher uses descriptive content analysis to describe students', staff's and institutions' participation and cooperation in various projects. The researcher also uses the same approach to investigate if these Palestinian higher education institutions intersect and share the research theme of whether Erasmus+ projects have a tangible effect on higher education institutions and on enhancing intercultural communication in Palestine. Not only does the researcher look for similarities while analyzing the collected documents, but the researcher also looks to find out which universities seem to be different. After dividing the documents to three levels, the researcher depending on the research questions has formulated codes and themes that enable her to answer the research questions. The following table presents these codes and themes

3.6 A Guide of the Analysis

	Cooperation	**Socio-Cultural**	**Cultural Knowledge**	**Sustainable Cooperation**	**Cultural Interaction**
Individual	Ricardo an Italian student who has come to study in IUG	Fatma-lulu a disabled student who left Gaza to study at the University of Glasgow	ICM reciprocal mobility enhances student and staff intercultural	Saleh Qanzih a student at An-Najah University through his Master's degree at Lille	Rula Zughayar, a student at Birzeit University who has had the chance to enroll in Erasmus+ ICM mobility to study a

			skills, knowledge and exact competencies	University has bridged the relations between his host university and Nablus municipality in Palestine as being part of the project that aims at consolidating the urban planning and cultural heritage in Nablus and France	semester in Marburg University in Germany, said: "It was a new experience for me that led me to deal with a new culture and new environment. It also empowered my personality and self-autonomy and taught me how to take decisions without the interference of my parents"
Institutional	New modules and best practices has been adopted in Palestinian universities such as PBL, Flipped-Classrooms and MooCs	New center has opened in Nablus due to an agreement between the Director of An-Najah Montessori Kindergarten and Stavanger University in Norway through E+ staff exchange mobility	Bethlehem University sends their staff to different EU countries to share experience and transfer knowledge to Palestine and transform the skills they learn to adapt them to suit the Palestinian universities providing the best quality training	METHODS project is one of the CBHE projects that have a sustainable effect through the implementation of the modalities at the Palestinian universities such as PBL, Flip-Classrooms and the Moocs	Improving the quality of higher education programs by initiating new Master joint agreement programs, dual and double degree system such as MS@ CPS

National	Four national repositories in four Palestinian universities the outcome of ROMOR project	The Ministry of HEIs and Scientific Research participate as a partner through E+ CBHE projects	Adopt innovative practices to ameliorate university governance in Palestine e.g UniGOV	The outcome of TAP CBHE project is having educational policies at the national level. A policy that calls for abandoning traditional assessment and using multi-assessment methodologies.	Involving an enterprise within the higher education sector has gained societies trust for Palestinian universities

Using themes and categorization has facilitated the process of analyzing the universities' material to answer the researcher's inquiries.

3.7. Conclusion

In this section, the researcher presents the approaches and methods utilized to answer the research questions and reach the overall aim of the study. The sample of the study, which represents 80% of the population of the study, is also mentioned. Moreover, EACEA's template form is used as an indicator for the researcher to map down and describe the impact of the selected Palestinian universities at three levels; the individual, the institutional and the national. The researcher concludes this section by providing a detailed description of the process she utilizes in analyzing her data.

Chapter Four

Results and Analysis

Chapter Four

Results and Analysis

4.1. Preview

After applying the tool and using the qualitative approach, the researcher, in this chapter, presents the results of the study with their analysis.

4.2. Results Related to the Study Questions

4.2.1 Erasmus+ Higher Education Aid Enhances Intercultural Communication

The researcher desk works the gathered documents that have been accumulated from seven Palestinian universities which are: Birzeit University (BZU), An-Najah National University (ANNU), Hebron University (HU), Bethlehem University (BU), Islamic University of Gaza (IUG), University College of Applied Sciences (UCAS) and Al-Azhar University in Gaza (AUG). In order to measure the impact of the Erasmus+ projects on these universities, the researcher uses the section of the impact in EACEA template both the ICM Flash Report and CBHE Field Monitoring. In ICM Flash Report, the researcher uses the following two conditions to measure the success of ICM mobility:

- The dissemination of mobility projects results
- The best practices that are transferred to individual home institutions

There are other conditions, yet these two conditions serve the purpose of the study. The researcher applies these two conditions on the information gathered from the seven universities to see if these conditions are implemented on their ICM mobility students and staff and, accordingly, the researcher states the following results:

- Erasmus+ has enhanced the individuals' personal development through cultural interaction.
- Individuals are more resilient, have strong personalities and are accountable for decision making.
- They have adopted the intercultural competent skills, entrepreneurship and innovative skills.
- They have been taught new pedagogical skills, methods and techniques such as PBL to face life gaps and apply these techniques in real life.
- Staff have disseminated the adapted skills and tools of teaching and learning to their universities, thus facilitating graduates' professional life.
- The mobility has fostered the individuals' research capacity through the cooperation with new colleagues from other universities, the thing that resulted in having more research outputs in Palestine leading to scientific publication.
- Employment rate has been accelerated due to Erasmus+ enrollment.
- Professional capacities are built and communication skills are enhanced.
- The cooperation and integration of HEIs, students and enterprise has facilitated the students' future career.
- Erasmus+ prioritizes the role of social inclusion through education.

These results show that the Palestinian universities under the enrollment of Erasmus+ programme have succeeded in implementing EACEA's two conditions in the ICM Flash Report. Concerning the ICM mobility, the best practices are disseminated to the Palestinians institutions internationalizing these institutions. The sub-questions elaborate more in depth on Erasmus+ activities in the targeted universities.

In the Field Monitoring, the researcher uses the indicators of the impact section to measure the implementation of the targeted universities to EACEA's conditions on CBHE projects. That is to see if the Palestinian universities, through their CBHE projects, have succeeded to implement EACEA's rules for a sustainable project that leads to the unexpected outcomes and more international collaboration.

The indicators at the individual level:

- The impact of enrollment rate or career development
- Prioritizing vulnerable groups (disadvantaged, special needs, refugees)

Due to the improvement in soft skills, social skills and employability skills that Erasmus+ ICM individuals acquire from their mobility, some of the students were assigned to work at the Ministry of Higher Education and Scientific Research after their graduation. Moreover, the Palestinian universities have incorporated enterprises that support students' practical placement, entrepreneurship and accelerate the employability of graduates. BZU is one example of the Palestinian universities which signed a university- enterprise agreement. The international networking in the field of research has elevated the Palestinian research capacity to meet the international standard. These researchers have found a job in their domain. Moreover, the ROMOR project is an example of Erasmus+ CBHE projects that preserve Palestinian scholar research in a repository. It is implemented in four Palestinian universities and has an aim to build a national repository. This shows that the Palestinian universities involved in Erasmus+ projects are internationalizing their universities and seeking to lessen unemployment rate in Palestine.

Erasmus+ prioritizes disadvantaged and marginalized students in their mobility interaction. Some disadvantaged students in Palestinian universities have joined Erasmus+ ICM mobility. This shows that the targeted Palestinian universities, which represent a sample of the Palestinian universities which enroll in Erasmus+ projects, have implemented EACEA's condition in prioritizing the marginalized category in Erasmus+ enrollment.

The indicators at the Institutional level:

- The project results into new courses/ strategies, services/ impact beyond the project team
- New national cooperation activities/ research projects/ joint publications have been launched in the partner country PC HEIs as a result of the project
- New international cooperation activities/ international agreements/ research projects/ joint publications in networks or associations have been launched in the PC HEIs as a result of the project.

Some of CBHE projects have an unexpected outcome. The seven sample of CBHE projects that the researcher has used have an impact beyond their projects. New cooperation has occurred and new proposal calls have been sent to Erasmus+ and are waiting for the results. The researcher provides a deep analysis on the unexpected outcomes of the targeted projects in an interview conducted with the coordinators of the projects. These interviews are located in the sub-questions results and analysis. New methodologies have been adapted and courses have developed accordingly. The "Flipped classroom" technique and "Problem-based learning" technique are implemented now at the Palestinian universities that are enrolled in Erasmus+ CBHE projects. Due to METHODs project, for example, new centers are opened in every university that cater for the education process with incubating modern technology. Moreover, new lab centers have been established at the Palestinian universities. Furthermore, new Master joint degrees, dual and double degree system have been initiated.

New national cooperation activities include:

- By product cooperation between Palestinian universities/joint research such as the inter- institutional joint research agreement between Coventry University and An-Najah National University
- By product cooperation between Palestinian faculties; for example, BZU has integrated interdisciplinary faculties to cooperate together in health informatics scientific research/ IT PENS project
- The university-enterprise linkage that bridges the socio-economic gap and accelerate employability rate (BZU/ Izhiman company)
- The cooperation between public HEIs, on one hand, and the public and private HEIs on the other hand.
- The private sector is considered for the first time as a part in developing the universities' curricula to meet the market needs.
- The formation of a coordination body that fosters the links between public/ private sectors and HEIs for the first time in Palestine.
- The involvement of the Ministry of Higher Education and Scientific Research as a partner in the project improves the governance of the universities by adapting new dual system, double degree system and joint Master degrees, thus increasing academic

programmes. An example for the joint Master project is MS in Cyber Physical System (MS@CPS).

- The initiation of new Master's programmes in Palestine for the first time such as, intellectual property, forensic computing and cyber-crimes.

New international cooperation activities include:

- New CBHE projects have emerged from the main projects as an unexpected outcome and are still waiting for the European acceptance. For example, MEE is an unexpected outcome that has been initiated beyond TAP project. More details are provided in sub-questions analysis.
- Nine new Master programmes have been established.
- New innovative education programmes have been established in Bachelor's, Master's and PhD level.
- The implementation and the adaptation of new modules, best practices and techniques in Palestinian universities such as PBL, Flipped Classrooms and MOOCs (example: METHODs project/ BZU, ANNU universities).
- The implementation of E-port, IT centers, repositories and industry liaisons offices (ILOs) (example for repositories: ROMOR project).
- The implementation of digital and modern learning methods.
- The implementation of the e-learning initiative that bridges educational and socio-political gaps, develops new curricula and integrates technology (example: TEFL-ePAL project).
- Knowledge transfer and networking with European universities leads to high quality education in new fields on the Bachelor's, Master's and PhD level.

- The promotion of research capacities by encountering foreign colleagues who have increased the research outputs in Palestinian universities and have led to scientific publications.
- The adaptation of the European best practices has increased the trust in Palestinian universities that are involved in Erasmus+ projects; therefore, it has elevated the Palestinian universities in QS ranking.
- The establishment of new laboratory facilities in Palestinian universities.
- The private sector is considered for the first time as a part in developing the universities curricula to meet the labor market needs.
- The acceleration of employability rate among the graduates of local universities.

The indicators that show the impact on the society as a whole (national level) are:

- The extent to which the project has paid particular attention to least developed regions/ countries.
- The extent to which the project contributes to engaging in new cooperation modalities with employers and other stakeholders (e.g. NGOs, associations etc.).
- The extent to which the project contributes to improving lifelong learning approaches in the PC HEIs.

One of Erasmus+ conditions and aim is to promote their programme in least developed countries or regions. Due to the fact that Palestine is an occupied country which lacks the possession of financial and other resources, Erasmus+ programme is concerned with elevating the Palestinian universities and promoting the lifelong learning process through the European and Palestinian cooperation and endeavors. Moreover,

Erasmus+, through its CBHE projects with the HEIs, non HEIs, NGOs and other associations, aims at promoting the lifelong learning process.

An example of the cooperation between Erasmus+ and one of the NGOs organizations is a project that encompasses Erasmus Tempus and CARE institution. The latter is a center for applied research in education. CARE is a non-profit voluntary institution whose objective is to set activities that lead to the promotion of the civic society. TEMPUS IV is CBHE project that encompasses Erasmus TEMPUS and CARE institution to enhance the quality of life learning capacities in HEIs, and non-university partners in Palestine with the association of programme/ partner universities and other centers. The project's aim is to expand the lifelong learning projects to society as a whole (Safi. 2012).

Moreover, Erasmus+ projects have succeeded in enabling Palestinian universities to adapt new methodologies, techniques, and educational programmes in Bachelor's, Master's, and PhD programmes through the excessive workshops, seminars, trainings, continuous CBHE projects, and the involvement of different stakeholders from the HEIs, NGOs, and other associations including mainly the Ministry of Higher Education and Scientific Research in some of CBHE projects as a partner. The role of the Ministry of Higher Education and Scientific Research improves the governance and management of the Palestinian universities. Therefore, Erasmus+ has succeeded in promoting the lifelong learning process through the sustainability of the education process which elevates the quality of teaching and learning at the Palestinian universities.

By introducing EACEA's indicators, the researcher has proved that enrolled Palestinian universities with Erasmus+ CBHE projects have implemented and applied all

EACEA's indicators conditions. Moreover, ICM conditions were also implemented. These have been the results, and they are explained in depth in the sub-questions section with more analysis, examples of CBHE projects, the target sample of the Palestinian universities, interviews with the director of Erasmus+ and interviews with Erasmus+ CBHE coordinators, and also the experiences of ICM mobilities at the Palestinian universities.

To sum up, the Erasmus+ educational aid and the overall sustainable enhancement of the Palestinians' and the Europeans' synergies have upgraded the QS ranking of the Palestinian universities through building strong capacities and indulging in joint research activities and new educational programmes.

4. 3. Results Related to the Study Sub-Questions:

4.3.1. Erasmus+ Strengthens Cooperation and Intercultural Communication

Erasmus+ helps and strengthens the cooperation and intercultural communication to a large extent whether in ICM mobility where mutual cooperation occurs between the programme and the partner countries or in CBHE projects. This cooperation occurs among students from partner and program countries from one side and between them and their staff from another side. Students in partner countries learn new techniques from the European universities. Moreover, cooperation in CBHE projects encompass the cooperation at:

- Inter-institutional cooperation at the national level
- Intra-institutional cooperation among university faculties
- International cooperation or regional cooperation

- The involvement and cooperation of local market companies to bridge the gap between the academia and the market place.

The results are followed by the analysis:

Erasmus+ conceptualizes the notion of cooperation throughout its entire European funded programme. Through key-action 1, students and staff mobilize from partner to programme countries and vice versa. They encounter diversified cultures and explore their people more deeply. Students become acquainted with people in European Countries to understand their way of thinking, their values and behaviors. Through cooperation and interaction with other cultures, students become interculturally competent. On the personal level, while experiencing a new lifestyle, these students become independent and develop strong personalities. Moreover, Erasmus+ has strengthened these students' language skills and knowledge about other countries and cultures. Students have improved their soft skills and interpersonal skills through ICM mobility. These skills are built through interaction with others and become beneficial to them in their placements. On the academic level, Erasmus+ enhances the students' personal traits and academic merit through adapting new techniques and methods. The individuals capture new knowledge and new information to be transmitted to their home universities. They learn foreign languages to ease their proficiency in communication with other cultures. Moreover, they gain competency through their interaction with other students and by mutual cooperation, too. Therefore, Erasmus+ projects theme is to cooperate and benefit from each other to be interculturally competent.

The transnational staff mobility, on the other hand, urges in accelerating the reciprocal connection by adapting new topics from other colleagues. These new topics benefit both the institutions and the students as well. They widen their research horizon and, therefore, lead to scientific publication and upgrade the level of the universities. Students, on the other hand, are exposed to new critical thinking techniques that they transfer to their institutions.

Despite the benefits of Erasmus+ ICM programme on the individual, Palestine, as a partner country, has its own specificity. Palestine faces a lot of obstacles concerning mobilities. The word mobility contradicts with the status quo of Palestine. For example, Gaza strip is under a total obstruction or siege which prevents Palestinians to easily obtain a visa or a permit. A visa for a Gazan student takes six months to apply prior travel which sometimes hinder him/her from starting their mobility on time. Furthermore, Erasmus+ enhances the spirit of challenge among its beneficiaries. Although Gaza is under blockade, Erasmus+ ICM selectees challenge their situation until they can join Erasmus+ mobility exchange programme. For example, Ahmad Albuhais, a Gazan citizen from the Islamic University in Gaza, has finally enrolled in Erasmus+ ICM exchange programme after a complicated visa issue due to the Israelis' procedures in blocking Gaza from the outside world. For him, this opportunity has opened his mind to new horizons (National Erasmus Office in Palestine, 2019). He has got a scholarship for a Master's degree to the university of Oldenburg in Germany after finishing his Bachelor's in computer engineering at the Islamic University in Gaza. Albuhais says:

> This so far was the best experience I had in my life. It changed me to the better; personally, and professionally. I learned many new things, got the opportunity to use very new advanced technologies, worked on real projects for well-known companies, and became a very qualified big data engineer.

Ahmad has also learned to speak German and met people from different cultures.

Another example that illustrates cooperation among Erasmus+ programme is the reciprocation of the incoming mobility to Palestine. This reciprocation assures the cooperation that occurs between partner and programme universities whether for outgoing or incoming students. Nargiz Mammadova is another incoming student mobility to Palestine from Azerbaijan and a Master's student at Siena University in Italy. During the visa procedure, she got denied entrance to the Palestinian territories since she is going to an Arab university. But with the interference of the European Union, her dream came into light. She came to Palestine on the 30th of January, 2019 and enrolled in the cultural diplomacy programme. Mammadova says that Erasmus+ was a turning point in her life that contributed to expanding her vision of the world. During her 3 months-stay at Birzeit University, she perceived people's hospitality and was fascinated by the Palestinians' rich cuisine. Moreover, her part-time job has helped her integrate with the Palestinian culture. This opportunity has helped shape her character as a person. Her stay in Palestine has also strengthened her inter-personal traits and built up her self-confidence and autonomy (Birzeit University, 2019).

AL-Azhar University of Gaza is another Palestinian university who has participated in Erasmus+ programme and has impact on its students and staff through ICM mobilities. At the personal level, Erasmus+ programme opens the mind of the students to be tolerant and acceptable to other people's differences. It motivates the students to develop their social skills and become aware of the European culture. At the academic level, on the other hand, students capture the nature of the educational system in the European countries and upgrade their English language skills. Through interaction, they have gained new knowledge and wide experience. Moreover, being exposed to lecturers and experts who have supported them with innovation skills has encouraged students to do research. Students have become entrepreneurs, the thing that has paved their way to professional career.

Through presenting some examples of ICM mobilities, the researcher assures that Erasmus+ plays a tremendous role in integrating different cultures together. This integration leads to multilateral cooperation and enables individuals to become interculturally competent and, thus, have a successful cross-cultural communication.

Moreover, Key Action 2 (CBHE), on the other hand, plays a visible and tangible role in illustrating Erasmus+ participation in enhancing cooperation and intercultural communication.

Knowing that every Palestinian university has its own educational system and lives in isolation from the others, Erasmus+, with its enormous programme, seeks to unify the Palestinian universities objectives to serve society as a whole. From the onset of Erasmus+ CBHE projects, cooperation is a key factor to success. The main aim of the European Union is to establish cooperation between the South and the North of the Mediterranean Region and such mutual cooperation between Europe as a programme country and Palestine as a Partner country is a great manifestation of this ensued cooperation. However, other by-product cooperation has resulted from the international cooperation since it is a prerequisite of having cooperation. Thus, the cooperation encompasses three levels, inter-institutional at a national level, intra-institutional among university faculties, and international cooperation or regional cooperation. In the inter-institutional level, the cooperation occurs between various Palestinian universities for instance, Birzeit and Hebron University, or with other regional ones under an international guidance. For example, the OpenMed project is a collaborative project that focuses on the cooperation of local Palestinian institutions such as Birzeit University and An-Najah National University with other regional universities such as Morocco, Egypt and Jordan. The aim of the project is to expand the participation and adoption of the Open Educational Resources to modernize the higher education institutions. It also seeks to elevate the quality of education and teaching by upgrading the teachers' competency.

Therefore, the project has its impact on different levels. It has built human resources by developing the skills of the staff. The project has also improved the educational practices of the local universities staff in order to gain new techniques and skills. Students, therefore, benefit from their teachers' experience. This cooperation occurs through using "flipped classrooms" techniques to engage students in blended cooperative learning. Through the blended learning, students participate together and come up with solutions if they face any obstacle by using the problem-based learning. These techniques upgrade the skill capacity of the students to face market place obstacles in the long run. Staff have been incorporated in national, international and virtual training to improve their skills. Moreover, participants have been involved in international cooperation activities such as curriculum and course design. At the institutional level, cooperation among Palestinians universities has occurred to implement OpenMed project. Finally, at the international level, an inter-institutional agreement has been initiated between Coventry University in UK and An-Najah NationalUniversity in Palestine to facilitate teaching through the exchange of qualitative research and academic writing. This exchange has been implemented at An-Najah National University through various international workshops. However, this cooperation cannot succeed unless the international intervention prevails. Thus, this project illustrates the multilateral cooperation at the national, regional and international level. Moreover, to know more about any project, the researcher provides more details on every utilized project in the attached annex.

There is also an intra-institutional cooperation among university faculties. For example, every faculty has its own cultural parameters that differ from one another. Also, the scientific research differs from one faculty to another. It is also worth mentioning that these faculties have never cooperated before. Therefore, Erasmus+ unintentionally and by product has played a significant role in expanding the cooperation among students from different faculties by joining them to accomplish assigned research projects. For instance, Birzeit University has integrated interdisciplinary faculties to cooperate together. The health sector and the information technology department have cooperated together to keep in pace with technological acceleration. This cooperation has bridged the gap between Birzeit University and the market place to pave the way for students' future career. Through these multilateral cooperation, Erasmus+ internationalizes education and never privatizes it to a certain specialization to cope with the industrial development which eventually lessens unemployment rate in Palestine.

At the international level, Erasmus+ CBHE and ICM mobilities are all being implemented under the supervision of EACEA and the European Union. The international cooperation strengthens the relations between the European and the Palestinian HEIs. EACEA's principle according to its indicators is based on an overall cooperation. Any project must include partners from programme countries and partners from partner countries to initiate cooperation among them. The cooperation, therefore, might be on the national and/or regional level with the international European countries. In the implementation phase of any CBHE project, work packages are distributed according to the needs and competencies of the institutions. The aim of the work package is to define and analyze the responsibilities of each partner institution in the project and distribute it among them according to their specialization and their available expertise. This sharing and cooperative process guarantees the execution of the project on its specific time unless unexpected obstacle traverses its process. Moreover, the kick of meeting of any project is also built upon cooperation. There are monthly online meetings and annual face-to-face meetings. Erasmus+ in the CBHE design stipulates that partners must be from different places to promote diversity among them. The distribution of work packages guarantees the exchange of experience among universities in order for every university to benefit from the other. Therefore, all Erasmus+ projects depend on the degree of participation of all the partners in the implementation of the project. The European Universities with their immense experiences help Palestinian counterparts to design the courses and the curriculum.

Erasmus+ cooperation has expanded to involve companies from the market place to collaborate in the development of the Palestinian curricula. For example, in the field of business and economic, Birzeit university has established a cooperation agreement with Izhiman Coffee Company to develop the curriculum and provide training and internship opportunities for students and graduates. This cooperation bridges the gap between academia and the market place to reduce the unemployment rate in Palestine (Ckeshek, 2020).

The researcher describes the impact of Erasmus+ CBHE projects at An-Najah National University to show how cooperation is illustrated. Exchanging research with European partners has assisted in strengthening the staff capability of writing researches. These mutual interactions have boosted academic relationships between programme country universities and An-Najah National University to work together and adopt new knowledge and specialization. New methodologies have emerged to be implemented in An-Najah National University. Teaching and training workshops are held to benefit from other partners and eliminate the social differences between different countries. Through mutual staff visits, An-Najah staff have learned how courses are being taught to enhance their courses delivery and assessment. They have also learned to update their existing labs or get the exact specification for a new lab.

A study conducted by the project team of the European Union (2019) interlaces with this sub-question. Both agree that Erasmus+ projects with its multilateral cooperation has renovated the curricula and pedagogical skills in Europe and Palestine, improved the intercultural competent skills of both student and staff, enhanced the relations with others by adapting new techniques to be used in their own country or region and finally increased the chance of employability.

4.3.2. Erasmus+ Bridges the Socio-Cultural Gap between the Higher Education System in the Palestinians and European Institutions

- Erasmus+ bridges the socio-cultural gaps between the higher education system in the Palestinian and the European institutions through: Erasmus+ set out an orientation day that precedes the ICM students' departure the thing that it reduces and bridges the socio-cultural gaps.
- Erasmus+ prioritizes marginalized students who have less opportunities in gaining their higher education level. / one of EACEA's conditions to be implemented to have a successful project.
- Erasmus+ diffuses equity among its ICM participants.

- The enrolled Erasmus+ Palestinian universities such as IUG incubates disabled students/ examples are listed in the analysis part. /
- Erasmus+ mends the gap of cultural identity through ICM mobility. /examples are in details in the analysis part. /
- Erasmus+ ICM students explore cultural changes. / taking An-Najah National University as an example.

The results are followed by the analysis:

Erasmus+ takes into consideration the socio-cultural factors that affect the thoughts, feelings and behaviors of their individual selectees. Some of these factors include; cultural deprivation, cultural identity, cross-cultural differences, attitudes, values, cultural change and finally the religious beliefs and practices. Erasmus+ bridges all these socio-cultural factors gaps through ICM mobilities. In general, Erasmus+ precedes the ICM mobilities' departure with an orientation day that gives students and staff feedback on their application process and the host country they are exposed to. Therefore, this activity reduces and bridges the socio-cultural gap that might face the ICM participants. In its enormous programme, Erasmus+ prioritizes deprived, disadvantaged, disabled and marginalized students who have less opportunities in gaining their higher education level. Erasmus+ seeks to implement its strategy for inclusion and diversity. It diffuses equity among its participants. Moreover, it strengthens them with knowledge, skills and behaviors to promote differences in society.

The Islamic university of Gaza is one of the Palestinian universities who has participated in Erasmus+ programme and has an impact on its students and staff through ICM mobilities. Although there is a good quantity of students who have participated in

ICM mobilities, less fortunate students with different disabilities had their share, too. Fatma Lulu, a disabled Gazan student in the Islamic University of Gaza, studied English literature and got accepted in the University of Glasgow in the UK for three months. Fatma says that this opportunity was a turning point in her life, too. Her skills have been developed and she has been exposed to methods of teaching which helped her improve her domain of studies. Consequently, she has become self- confident and got the chance to present herself and speak in front of Scottish people, the thing that enhanced her self-autonomy. Moreover, Fatma's disability did not prevent her from getting along with others. On the contrary, she built strong relationships and made close friends. Glasgow's people were intimate, social and loyal, Fatma concludes (Erasmus+ Programme, 2019).

Another example is an impaired student who has benefited from the international credit mobility in Erasmus+ programme. Sa'di Abu Amra is an MA student at the Islamic University of Gaza. Although he suffers from hearing impairment, his deafness did not prevent him from pursuing his dream and benefiting from the ICM grant. Due to his disability issue, Abu Amra got rejected from different universities. They have claimed that it will be difficult for him to communicate with lecturers. After long negotiations, the Islamic University enrolled him to complete his Master's degree. Through his education journey, he got selected to join the ICM mobility despite his hearing impairment. He has studied for eleven months at Humboldt University in Germany. He says that: "I am grateful for providing a number of sign language interpreters to facilitate communication with people with disabilities through sign language. I (am) also filled with gratitude for using technology in studying the German sign language" (National Erasmus Office in Palestine). Sa'di concludes that, due to impairment facilities provided by the university, he has integrated into the German society and has made new friends who shared the same disability. He also has given religious lectures to people of hearing disabilities in a mosque in Berlin. Without the chance of enrollment with Erasmus+ mobility, he has not had the chance to engage with other cultures and mingle with other people.

A related study conducted by Cinotti et al. (2018) seeks to equalize education and tackle disadvantaged and disabled students. It aims at improving learning conditions in higher education institutions for disabilities in order for them to have equal employment opportunities. This CBHE study shares the same aim of Erasmus+ which is bridging the socio-cultural gaps. Erasmus+ in Palestine, as presented by the experiences of ICM disability and impaired students, gives the priority of participation to marginalized and disadvantaged students. It implements the parameters of European Union which indicate the importance of choosing marginalized students in Erasmus+ mobility. Students from different Palestinian universities through ICM mobilities improve their interpersonal skills. They meet with other students abroad and cooperate with them in class and through project works. Through integration and cooperation with foreign students, Palestinian disabled students have overcome the socio-cultural gaps. Moreover, by sending disability students, the inter-institutional cooperation also plays a role in bridging the socio-cultural gaps. The partner and programme universities work together in building the disabilities' self-esteem by giving them the chance to participate in ICM activities regardless of their health condition. Therefore, Erasmus+ takes into consideration the students' psychological factors and gives students the ability to perform better in an environment other than their home institution and society. A disability person may be rejected by his home universities as shown in Sa'di's case in Gaza. He, after a lot of negotiations and due to his impairment disability, has been accepted in the Islamic university. Erasmus+ mobility has opened the horizon for him and the foreign institution has enhanced his self-esteem and independency. He got exposed to new techniques and methods that have helped him and other impaired students to engage well in society. Sa'di, therefore, was able to break the ice by mingling with others. He has felt culturally accepted and has functioned well abroad. Consequently, Erasmus+, in the case of Sa'di, has been able to bridge the cross-cultural differences. Moving to a new culture has not been an impediment in front of Sa'di's will. On the contrary, he has been able to adjust quickly by finding new acquaintance that shared with him his new experience.

Another socio-cultural gap is cultural identity. Erasmus+, with its enormous programme, tends to mend this gap. In the case of Palestine, students from the targeted universities and who participates in ICM exchange mobility explore cultural changes. Taking An-Najah National University as an example, outgoing students who travel abroad through Erasmus+ programme were resilient and tolerant to accept new cultures and exchange knowledge with foreign students. Before engaging in Erasmus+ programme, Ahmad AlBuhais, a Palestinian student from the Islamic University of Gaza, described his experience as being the best experience he has ever had in his life. His participation is reflected onto his personal traits and social cohesiveness. He learned Germany and was able to communicate with people from different cultures. Although he comes from a region that is under the Israeli siege and where communication with other cultures is somehow nonexistent, Al Buhais was able to integrate perfectly with the German culture.

This portion of the question intersects with a study conducted by Haj, K., & Erez (2018). The aim of the study was to explore the challenges that an Arab Muslim girl encountered while she was studying in Germany concerning her identity. The researchers of the study find that Erasmus+ has played a major role in transforming and reshaping the girl's cultural identity and that is by deconstructing her norms to fit within other cultures which made her express herself easily. So after six months of her journey, she was able to strike a balance between her family and religion and put limits to what she cannot accept. The study intersects with Erasmus+ aim which is to integrate and mingle with other cultures no matter what identities an individual possesses. Therefore, through illustrating the impact of the targeted universities and the ICM students' experiences, the researcher proves that Erasmus+ bridges the socio-cultural gaps perfectly in Palestine.

4.3.3. Erasmus+ Projects Contributes in Promoting Cultural Knowledge between Palestine and Europe

Erasmus+ projects surely contribute at a large scale in promoting and enhancing the cultural knowledge through:

- The ICM reciprocal mobility that enhances the student and staff intercultural skills, knowledge and exact competencies.
- The adoption of international methods such as flip-classrooms and problem-based learning which catalyzes team work (identifying METHODS as a related project).
- The adoption of international innovative practices to establish an adequate management system that upgrades the whole Palestinian education system (mentioning uniGOV as a related project).

The results are followed by the analysis:

Erasmus+, through its programme, aims at providing students, trainers, staff in universities with the fundamental intercultural skills, the knowledge they require and the exact competencies for interacting with international students. ICM selectees are offered new opportunities to explore new horizons. They become open-minded and tolerant to other people differences and aware of European cultures. ICM students develop their social skills by interacting with other students in team work projects. Their constant interaction with European professors and students helped their language skills to progress. Communicating with their European peers, Palestinian students build their self-confidence and self-esteem. On the academic level, Erasmus+ enriches Palestinian ICM students with new experiences that enable them to master research tasks well. Palestinian students have adopted new techniques and methods from their counterpart universities that have never been utilized at the Palestinian universities. Some of these techniques are the flipped classroom and problem- based learning technique where students are integrated together to share their knowledge and experiences among each other and try to find solutions on their own to any unexpected bottleneck. Moreover, METHODS an Erasmus+ CBHE project has adopted these two techniques from the European universities to be implemented in the Palestinian higher education institutions. It aims at raising the competencies of individual learners by promoting the learning process of the students to become an independent active learner. Furthermore, METHODS seeks to build the capacity of the Palestinian universities to assess, improve and design the e-curricula.

Hebron University is one of the universities that has participated in Erasmus+ ICM and CBHE projects and benefited from them. Students in this university have been able to accept diversity and differences in cultures. They also have accepted the values and traditions of the European countries. Moreover, they have become independent and more able to take on responsibilities and multi-task functions. On the academic level, they have been exposed to new methods that build their professional capacity on the long run.

These new methods urge them to think critically while solving any academic problem or life problem. Likewise, through Erasmus+ CBHE projects, Bethlehem University sends staff to different European countries to share their own experiences, transfer new knowledge to Palestine and transform the skills they learn to adapt them to suit the Palestinian universities providing the best quality training.

Incoming European students disseminate their universities knowledge with the Palestinian students, the thing that elevates their educational capacity and widens their thinking horizon. Moreover, these incoming students internationalize the institutions by joining and collaborating with the Palestinian students in writing mutual researches. This elevates the quality of the academic programs through implementing new international techniques that improve the quality of the curricula. On the other hand, the European incoming students benefit from their integration with Palestinian students and disseminate their experience back home.

Riccardo Corradin, an Italian student who has had the chance to join Erasmus+ exchange programme, comes from the university of Siena in Italy majoring in emergency surgery. He has enrolled in the Islamic university in Gaza. According to him, he reports that he has captured new techniques in surgery that he thinks have added to his knowledge. He has felt intimate with the Gazan people and felt at home. Moreover, Riccardo adds that his experience in Gaza was due to the huge casualties he encountered during the war which far exceed the casualties in Italy. Riccardo has transferred this experience to his colleagues in Italy to benefit from what he has learned in his Erasmus+ mobility (Ruptly, 2019).

Erasmus+ has helped the universities to improve and develop at different levels. It has established an adequate management system through adopting innovative practices from multinational countries to upgrade academic quality and the whole education system. UniGOV, is a national, regional and international cooperative CBHE project that addresses the weaknesses in the current governance system among the Palestinian higher education institutions. It aims at establishing a European- Palestinian framework that adopts the European innovative practices to ameliorate university governance in Palestine. Therefore, adopting innovative European practices adds to the Palestinian cultural knowledge. Thus, this clarifies and illustrates the role of Erasmus+ in enriching the Palestinians' cultural knowledge by the afore-mentioned efforts.

A study conducted by Bryla P. (2015) shows how Erasmus+ has helped the students to master a foreign language better than those students who did not participate. It also reveals that Erasmus+ mobility contributes to multiple skills and competencies. This related study overlaps with this sub-question by illustrating the role of Erasmus+ in elevating the Palestinian cultural knowledge through upgrading the individual skills and competencies by adopting international knowledge and accepting diversified cultures.

4.3.4. Erasmus+ Projects Yield Sustainable Cooperation

Erasmus+ projects are highly sustainable since the first condition in Erasmus+ acceptance of any CBHE project is to have some visible sustainability when submitting the proposal to Erasmus+. Moreover, by presenting some of Erasmus+ CBHE projects and interviewing their coordinators, the researcher has had a clear view about sustainability in every selected project. On the other hand, leaving students to take a course or two in a host university enhances sustainability and this is through signing the reciprocal agreement between home and host universities. This agreement is permanent thus generations of students keep enrolling in Erasmus+ ICM mobility.

The results are followed by the analysis:

Erasmus+ supports sustainable development in education. It contributes in making economic growth not only attainable but also sustainable by disseminating equity and quality in education and innovation jobs among its participants. Erasmus+, in Palestine and through its multilateral projects, focuses on enhancing and developing the human resources to benefit the Palestinian society at a national level. The most important condition in accepting any CBHE project in Erasmus+ programme is its sustainability meaning its continuation of the long-term benefit after the end of the project duration. In order to maintain the project results and according to EACEA's indicators in the Field Monitoring template, an adequate higher education institutions and external support are recommended. In order for a project to be a successful one, its impact must be sustainable on the long run and there are various ways to measure sustainability which are to be mentioned later.

As for ICM mobility, leaving students to take a course or so in the host institution enhances sustainability through signing a reciprocal agreement between the home and host institution. This agreement is continuous and permanent; thus, generations of students and from everywhere will enroll in Erasmus+ ICM mobility. Moreover, the institutions, by sending their staff to any host country, develop the staff competencies to transfer a good quality of education to their students. On the other hand, the Ministry of Education has a national and economical dimension. It obtains new educational methodologies and courses that suit the labor market needs. These long term agreements are approved by the accreditation and quality assurance commission (AQAC). They work hand in hand with the higher education institutions to improve the quality of higher education by imposing well- developed accreditation criteria that suit the Palestinian situation. The AQAC main asset is to invest in human capital to challenge the competitive world (AQAC Palestine, 2020).

ICM mobility at An-Najah NationalUniversity (ANNU) is one of the Palestinian universities that is still in permanence of fostering the ties between ANNU and other European universities. Ms. Nermin Habaybeh, the director of An-Najah Montessori Kindergarten and coordinator of Early Childhood Training Programmes at An-Najah Child Institute and through Erasmus+ exchange staff expertise programme has managed to sign a mutual agreement with Stavanger University in Norway to open a new training center. Through the staff exchange mobility, Habaybeh has built new personal and academic relations with the Stavanger University staff. These acquired competencies and transferred best practices have enabled her to have a mutual sustainable cooperation with Stavanger University.

Furthermore, Saleh Qanazih, a student at An-Najah National University, has completed his Master's degree at Lille University in France through Eramus+ ICM programme. During his period of study, he has bridged the relation between his host university and Nablus Municipality in Palestine as being part of the project that aims at consolidating the urban planning and cultural heritage in Nablus (Palestine) and Lille (France). Therefore, Qanazih's mobility has expanded his relations with his host University to build sustainable cooperation between the two countries. This cooperation is a lifelong cooperation and a continuous agreement that has its permanent proliferation (National Erasmus Office in Palestine).

CBHE projects have long term sustainable benefits throughout its stages of cooperation. The researcher mentions some of Erasmus+ CBHE projects that are run in Palestine and encompass partners from Palestinian universities and/ or regional ones from one hand and European Universities from the other hand shedding the light on its sustainable long-term effect. CBHE projects are either terminated projects with tangible sustainability or still ongoing projects with anticipated sustainability. Some CBHE projects integrate a labor market partner to ameliorate the curricula in order to bridge the gap between the educational institutions and the workplace. As aforementioned, all the CBHE projects that the researcher uses in the research are detailed in the provided annexes.

Pathway in Enterprise Systems Engineering (PENS) is an ongoing project that has Birzeit University as a coordinator with Al-Quds University being a partner. This project terminates in October 2020. The project aims at renovating the computing education by implementing Enterprise System Engineering to the IT program. Moreover, eight new courses have been introduced, by the same project, with the cooperation of Palestinian, Tunisian and European universities. PENS has also engaged private sectors to facilitate the training of students in order to bridge the gap of the market needs. These enterprises are Al- Andalus Software Development in Palestine and Proxym IT in Tunisia. Through this integration of the private sector, PENS plans to engage students in projects from start to finish by getting a full year internship to ensure the sustainability of the project and the market readiness of the students once they graduate. The project has a social and economic effect that assures its sustainability. The skills and competencies that PENS provides for students enhance their chances of employability and open access to new innovations and entrepreneurship. This project helps students to cope with and be aware of the alteration of the market needs whether nationally in Palestine or internationally. It is also expected to have quality of computer students that are ready for the labor market. The participant Palestinian institutions have accredited the eight new courses to be taught in their universities. This elevates the capacity building of the institutions by training the academics and the staff faculty through the project stage. The project is expected to have a wider effect on the industry and the IT sectors in Palestine. Accordingly, this project has a tripartite benefit. It benefits the individual, institution and the industrial place as well since individuals are now beneficial to the labor market. This illustrates that the sustainability of the project is a life time benefit.

The researcher has interviewed the coordinator of PENS project Dr. Yousef Hasooneh and asked him how he measures the sustainability of the project. He replied that through the current topics, sustainability can be measured. He added: "since we are talking about the knowledge of IT, we have to take into consideration its rapid acceleration in the world of technology. Therefore, the curriculum is dynamic and needs to be reformed and evolved every time". By reforming it periodically, sustainability is guaranteed. While interviewing, the researcher has asked the coordinator if there is any possible future cooperation between the regional or European institutions. Dr. Hasooneh revealed that BZU has already submitted a new proposal to Erasmus+ for a project with Spain and Italy as European partners, AL-Quds University as a national partner with the association of the Tunisian companies Proxym IT and Sousa; they are still waiting for the answer. The name of the two new projects are Digital Transformation and Cyber Security. The latter has new partners whose relations have been built through PENS project. These partners are Germany, Norway and Spain with Egypt being a regional partner and Al-Quds University a national one. Such cooperation and institutional relations show the continuity of the intercultural communication at all levels nationally, regionally and internationally.

Erasmus+ focuses on building the capacity of the individual to produce an active member that benefits society. Modernization of Teaching Methodologies in Higher Education (METHODS) aims at raising individual competencies through enhancing their learning process with new strategies of teaching in order to improve the quality of teaching and learning. It seeks to build the capacity of the partner countries universities since it is a national, regional sustainable project cooperation that connects Palestine, Jordan with The European Universities. METHODS trains the academic staff in the universities on how to assess, promote and design e-curricula. It is composed of four modalities:

- Competence-based teaching (CBT)
- Problem-based learning (PBL)
- Flipped Classroom
- Massive Open Online Course (MOOCs)

These modalities have been accredited by the Ministry of Education to be imposed and implemented at the Palestinian universities. Staff cannot be tenured or promoted to teach in the universities they desire unless these four tools are mastered. These modalities are implemented on students as well. They use these new modalities in their social and academic life to solve their problems.

In addition, a Memorandum of Understandings (MOUs) has been signed by different stakeholders to engage students in labor markets. The impact of this MOUs lasts as long as the modalities exist. Students have been collaborating and training with different companies such as, Israa and Spark company that has been involved in An-Najah National University teaching modality to sustain these modalities on the long run. In BZU, training sessions have been given to students for designing games and sensors based on the problem-based learning skill to solve any sudden problem. Accordingly, METHODs has been used to raise students' competencies by teaching them problem-based learning skill (PBL) to solve labor market problems. With these modalities, students have taken the responsibilities of analyzing problems, fixing meetings with external partners and analyzing data and surveys. This project has increased the employability rate; therefore, some students have worked at two companies and they have been able to use these methods in their work by finding solutions to problems they face. Thence, METHODs is a project that has its sustainable impact at the individual level by building the staff and student capacities and competencies.

Courses have been developed according to METHODs project. Inter-institutional experiences at the national level between Bethlehem University (BU) and Birzeit University (BZU) have been exchanged. BU have shared their experiences in applying PBL modality in business and education discipline since BZU focuses on engineering more than art. Moreover, four courses are conducted in each partner university and trainers disseminate their knowledge of modalities, the thing that guarantees the sustainability of these modalities on the long run. At An-Najah National University (ANNU), the academic staff have implemented METHODs modalities on literary criticism course for English department students. Palestine Polytechnic University (PPU), on the other hand, has given a workshop on the use of METHDs modalities sustaining its impact.

Moreover, the Islamic and Al-Aqsa universities in Gaza Strip have introduced METHODs modalities to be implemented in their institutions. Although the project has been executed on May 2019, new training sessions are still successive to introduce the new modalities, the thing that shows its sustainability effect. A bilateral agreement concerning the inter-institutional at the regional level has been signed between the Palestinian and the Jordanian higher education institutions to disseminate experiences. Two teaching and learning units have been established in the University of Jordan (UJ) and BZU by applying virtual learning to the four modalities. To sum it up, the project has its impact on the individual by building the capacity and the competency of students and staff. It also has its impact on the institutional level since it adjusts and renovate the curriculum at the partners' institutions, and the staff are being trained to teach these modalities at their institutions. Finally, the project has its impact on the national level since these modalities are accredited, to all universities, to be the criteria upon which designated staff are to be accepted. Students, on the other hand, get employed easily since they possess competencies that enable them to solve effectively any obstacle that crosses their work.

In an interview, Dr. Wasel Ghanem, the coordinator of METHODs project from BZU said: "students have to work together and collaborate to demonstrate a problem process, analyze an argument or apply a concept of a real world situation. The most important aim of the project is to avoid the lecturing style." When asking him if there are any future correlations beyond METHODs project between the Palestinian partner institutions and the European ones, Dr. Ghanem said that there are cooperation between the Palestinian partners and their colleagues in Denmark and Germany. He says: "we are in a phase of developing two new European projects that are follow-up to METHODs project. The first one is on how we can use PBL for engineering faculty students, and the second one is to integrate PBL in digital media." He added that it is very important to emphasize more on the PBL and give it its specificity and enhancement. Moreover, he focused on the role of PBL in enhancing the competencies of media students in order to follow up with the new digital technologies. Through initiating new projects, Dr. Ghanem assures that there is an ongoing cooperation between national, regional and international partners and which is a sustainable one.

To maintain sustainability among its projects, Erasmus+ seeks to improve the governance of the institutions. Thus, it is an integrated unit that focuses on ameliorating the whole higher education system. Due to the political situation, Palestinian higher education is considered weak and needs international intervention. Therefore, Erasmus+ CBHE project named Improving Governance Practices and Palestinian Higher Education Institutions (uniGOV), a project that involves the cooperation of Palestinian universities with European universities, improves the existing governing practices at the Palestinian universities and the quality of the higher education institutions in the Southern Mediterranean regions. The main aim is to establish a common governance framework through adopting innovative practices from the European countries to renovate academic quality and stimulate the five dimensions of the universities governance. The five dimensions are: autonomy, accountability, transparency in institutional tasks and goals, participation, and well- formed management systems to ensure the implementation of these practices.

In an interview with Dr. Mohamad Al-Najjar, the coordinator of uniGOV project in An-Najah National University, Dr. Al Najjar mentioned that before knowing what kind of training is needed and in what dimension, a diagnostic tool has been established to measure the degree of weaknesses since it differs from one university to another. He says: "based on the governance tool, we measured how well or bad we are in the different governance dimensions, and this was the base of our project". Moreover, he added that this tool is to be used further to measure the improvement of each dimension before moving to a new dimension. Virtual and face-to-face trainings have been set up for Palestinian university staff to attend. This has been done by the European universities where each university has specialized in specific fields and can give training courses in its specialization. Therefore, best practices have been transferred from Europe to Palestine, taking into consideration the different European frameworks regarding governance that do not fit in the Palestinian framework. In other words, Dr. Al-Najjar said "they (Palestinian universities) have adapted not adopted some governance system because it will not work in Palestine since we have a different culture, a different system, and different rules and regulations". During the interview the researcher asked Dr. Al-Najjar if he thinks the project yields sustainable cooperation. Dr. Al-Najjar said: "the diagnostic tool, the online materials, videos, face-to-face trainings and the staff who have trained are our sustainable outcome and can be used over and over again".

The researcher, then, asked the interviewee if uniGOV project has enhanced the intercultural communication between Palestinian and European higher education institutions.

Dr. Al-Najjar replied:

> New communications and relations with other universities have been developed from uniGOV project. An-Najah National University with the University of Siena have agreed upon introducing a joint Master degree in business and international

accounting. Moreover, there is a notion of launching ICM exchange students between University of Evora and the faculty of engineering in An-Najah National University. There are also new joint projects between An-Najah National University and University College Cork, University of Ljublijana and UNIMED (association of universities). These projects are virtual lab and internationalization.

This provides real examples of such an effect.

By presenting some of Erasmus+ projects, the researcher has found that sustainability has been planned for from the beginning of the project. The project has to have at least some sustainable outcomes when presenting the proposal before the initiation of the project. It might extend for a few years or for many years.

A study conducted by Mahauad et al. (2018) called the LALA project focuses on the academic side of the governance and complements the work of the uniGOV project which focuses on the governance of the management system. The LALA project aims at modernizing the academic administrative procedures through building the local capacity in order to create the learning analytics to support Latin America's higher education system. This ongoing project is assumed to have an impact at so many levels. As for the individual level, this project is to benefit both students and academic authorities. The latter are to implement the project strategy and tools in order to help understand diverse educational process since it is a mutual academic project cooperation between Europe and Latin America. Students, on the other hand, are expected to encounter innovative curricula that upgrade their educational system and modernize their course of learning through the implementation of learning analytic project techniques.

Regarding the local, regional and institutional level, adopted tools are designed to improve the higher education decision-making process on the local level. Nevertheless, at the regional level, it is disseminated to share its experience using the learning analytics in Latin America's higher education system. Whilst at the institutional level, a methodology is to be formed to adopt tools that can help to improve the learning process in higher education on a bigger scale. Finally, Europeans can benefit from the output of the project by distributing it to new partners that can benefit from them on their upcoming projects. As previously mentioned, the two projects complement each other and their sustainability is visible at all levels.

4.3.5. Erasmus+ Impact of Cultural Interaction between Higher Education Institutions at the Individual, Institutional and National Level

Cultural interaction has a positive impact on individuals represented by outgoing and incoming ICM students and staff. Not only does this mutual interaction help in building the competencies and capacities of the individuals, but it also enriches them with new knowledge, methods and procedures to be transmitted to their home institutions. The impact of Erasmus+ projects is an ongoing cycle. Students and staff disseminate their acquired knowledge at their home institutions which eventually is disseminated to large community of universities. Therefore, this helps in upgrading the whole Palestinian community.

The interaction at the Individual level manifests in:

- Building the intercultural competent skills, entrepreneurship and innovative skills for students and staff and exploring new experiences.

- Exploring new cultures and people which enriches students' and staff's personality by building self-confidence and having strong autonomy.
- Improving the quality of teaching and learning by introducing new pedagogical skills, techniques and methods to face life gaps
- Facilitating cooperation and integration of HEIs' students and enterprise to facilitate the students' future career.
- Enabling students to master foreign language and communication skills.

The cultural interaction at the Institutional level:

- Internationalizing Palestinian universities by adapting new techniques, new topics, and approaches such as PBL and diversified curricula which elevate the level of the universities.
- Learning how to enhance contents of the courses, how to deliver and assess them (TAP) project.
- Promoting sustainable networking through the elevation of research capacity to meet the internationalized standards (ROMOR).
- Improving the quality of higher education programmes by initiating new Master joint agreement programmes, dual and double degree system (MS in Cyber Physical).
- Integrating an outside stakeholder from labor market to ameliorate the courses to fit the market needs.
- Applying the e-learning modules to the modified curricula, the thing that keeps the students convoy to technology and accelerates employment rates.
- Strengthening the national, regional and international relations.

The cultural interaction at the National level:

- New horizons are open to society by accepting transferred knowledge.
- Competitiveness among Palestinian universities staff due to cooperation and international exchange of experience which increased employability.
- Students possession of high competency in research projects which elevates the rank of the universities and is suitable for labor market in the area of research management.
- Erasmus+ projects best practices are implemented at the Palestinian universities.
- The involvement of the Ministry of Higher Education and Scientific Research improves the governance of the universities by adapting new dual system, double degree system and joint Master degrees, thus increasing academic programmes.
- Erasmus+ projects play a role in elevating the QS ranking of Palestinian universities.
- Involving an enterprise within the higher education sector has gained societies' trust for Palestinian universities.

The results are followed by the analysis:

Erasmus+, through ICM and CBHE, projects strives to provide the higher education institutions represented by students and staff with beneficial tools to improve their competencies and capacities, thus improving the profile of their institution. When arriving to their host country, ICM students interact with other university students to develop their cultural awareness. They become acquainted with this new culture and familiar with its norms and values. In the classroom, they interact with their classmates and learn their language. They also learn new methods and techniques that enable them to transfer them to their home universities. Therefore, the home universities adopt the new methods to be implemented according to their needs. The whole ICM process is built on cultural interaction. Students from different faculties are gathered together to pilot

Erasmus+ experience. They come from different backgrounds, different cultures and study different disciplines, yet they are united under Erasmus+ exchange mobility period.

Staff from different universities are also culturally mingled with their mates from other universities. They exchange experiences with each other through training sessions or workshops. They learn new strategies to be implemented in their home institutions.

CBHE projects, on the other hand, encompass cultural interaction since they are based on the cooperation and correlation of partner countries universities with their programme countries counterparts. There are inter-institutional national and sometimes regional cultural interaction and that depends on the project and its partners with the international intervention. The partners who participate in launching a project interact together and share their experiences with each other. Cultural interaction starts from the initiation period of the project and the distribution of work packages. Each university selects its specification and all the partners exchange experiences among them. Once the Palestinian partners are exposed to virtual, face-to-face trainings with their European counterparts, they transfer knowledge to their home universities. Wherefore, Erasmus+ ICM and CBHE projects build the capacities and competencies of their individuals by transferring the best practices from the European universities to upgrade and ameliorate the higher education institutions. This cultural interaction has an impact on the individual, the institution itself and the whole nation.

The Impact of the Cultural Interaction at the Individual Level (ICM&CBHE):

Erasmus+ ICM mobility plays a crucial role in enriching students' and staff's personality. While traveling abroad and interacting with other individuals from other cultures whether at work or universities, individuals' personalities develop. It encourages them to have self-confidence with strong autonomy in order to take any personal decisions without patriarchal intervention.

Rula Zughayar, a student at Birzeit University who has had the chance to enroll in Erasmus+ ICM mobility to study a semester in Marburg University in Germany, said: “It was a new experience for me that led me to deal with a new culture and new environment. It also empowered my personality and self- autonomy and taught me how to take decisions without the interference of my parents” (National Erasmus Office in Palestine, 2019).

Moreover, students have been able to adapt to new cultures, interact and integrate with their people. Through cultural integration and cooperation among different cultures, individuals’ cultural shock is reduced. The students’ entrepreneurship and innovation skills are promoted to carve their paths in professional graduate life. They are being exposed to new techniques and methods and acquainted with new knowledge. They have also experienced new foreign languages that enable them to communicate with foreign cultures and develop their academic merit. The students have advanced their interpersonal skills, and the exchange mobility has enhanced their research ability writing.

Rafeef Quzmar, a student at Birzeit University, has attended Erasmus+ ICM mobility. She says: “I went to Philips University in Germany. I learned how to write a research project in a new developed way and came back home and taught my colleagues” (National Erasmus Office in Palestine, 2019).

Moreover, students have been resilient to accept new cultures and interchange knowledge with other students. They have been able to work in teams and use new methods to solve any sudden problems. ICM mobility has helped students to develop their competencies to compete in the global market. As mentioned before, METHODs is one of the CBHE projects that enhances competencies by teaching students new modalities such as flip classrooms and problem-based learning to help them face any sudden problem in class and also in life. Students have been able to think critically leading them to creativity. According to ICM cultural interaction, Bethlehem University (BU) has been able to participate in learning, entrepreneurship, and job shadowing workshops and conferences across Europe. The METHODs project has raised the competencies of BU individual learners to be active members through incorporating technological tools with pedagogical best practices.

Incoming scholars to Palestine have benefited the Palestinian students with new research and training. They enhance collaborative network with the Palestinians higher education institutions through building international relations with academics and professionals. This cultural interaction is built either through joint projects or joint scientific researches. The outgoing staff, on the other hand, integrate with the host universities and adapt new international methods that enhance teaching at their home institutions. CBHE staff participation in international training has simultaneously benefited students through the use of computer labs, developed teaching materials that contain e-learning material and other international tools.

To sum it up, cultural interaction has a positive impact on individuals represented by outgoing and incoming ICM students and staff. Not only does this mutual interaction help in building the competencies and capacities of the individuals, but it also enriches them with new knowledge, methods and procedures to be transmitted to their home institutions. The European integration increases the Palestinians' awareness of soft and digital skills in the teaching process.

The Impact of Cultural Interaction at the Institutional Level:

Cultural interaction among the higher education institutions enhances the quality of these institutions. The transnational staff mobility urges in accelerating the reciprocal connection by adapting new topics from European colleagues. This transferred knowledge widens the Palestinians' HEIs research horizons and, therefore, leads to scientific publications. It also ameliorates the level of the universities. Students are exposed to new critical thinking techniques and problem-based learning approaches which they transfer to their universities and are used in solving real life problems. The aim of Palestinian institutions is to internationalize their universities academically. They usually choose partner institutions that add value to their universities, diversify their curricula and guarantee a good quality of education for students and staff. CBHE projects help staff to renovate part of the curricula and teaching materials. They aid in establishing new labs and develop specialized trainings. Through their participation in CBHE projects, new cooperation and endeavors are held upon national, regional and international institutions. The mutual interactions with the European universities boost academic relationships between both the programme and the partner country universities. These interactions seek to improve the quality of teaching and learning through ameliorating and updating the curricula. They also provide and update the Palestinian institutions with new knowledge and specializations. They grant the Palestinian universities staff the chance to explore new methodologies and pedagogical approaches to be implemented and introduced in their universities. They learn how European staff teach their courses and observe the materials and the courses they teach, how the European faculties interact with their students, and review their lab experiments. They also create or modify lab centers and enhance contents of the courses the European teach while learning how to deliver and assess them.

A CBHE project named TAP, which is Transforming Assessment Practices in higher education in Palestine, is based upon using technology and employing it in learning assessment. It aims at using formative assessment along with summative one. Dr. Abdel Karim, the coordinator of this project in An-Najah NationalUniversity, gives more details about this project. Through an interview, he said: "before giving students grades, you give them many opportunities to improve their learning achievements and learning habits and practices". He added that students learn while they are being assessed. After explaining a certain concept for a certain methodology, for instance, students are being asked a question to make sure that they got the concept. Technology is being used alongside the curricula. Twelve pilot courses have been designed using that methodology in the TAP project. Dr. Abdel Karim revealed that: "these methodologies are implemented at An-Najah National University in Biology and Calculus courses. The biology course Genetics and Society last call won An-Najah E-learning award for 2019-2020". So, this cultural interaction has resulted from the implementation of specific online materials and courses, the thing that assures its sustainability. The TAP project has opened future communication with the European higher education institutions. When asking Dr. Abdel Karim if there are any new intentions for future projects that strengthen the Palestinian – European higher education relations, he replied: "We have applied for a new project called MEE which is Modernizing Education Engineering in Palestine". The continuation of collaboration with the European partners, he added, means the success of TAP implementation.

Moreover, research capacity is too elevated and upgraded to meet the internationalization standards. Due to the importance of researches and to help ensure the continuous access of these materials, the ROMOR project, Research Output Management Repository, has been established to preserve the research publications, the students' thesis (for example, PhD, Master thesis), raw data, and software through building institutional repositories. This project aims at preserving the intellectual properties of the universities in a digital form in order to give an exact number of research output rather than an approximate one which is far from reality. Capacity is built in how to define, maintain, preserve and sustain the partner institution repositories. When asking Dr. Rawia, the coordinator of ROMOR project at the Islamic University of Gaza, about how sustainability is measured in this project, she replied: "We have now the four institutional repositories running in the four partner universities and we are also implementing the policies on them and more people are depositing their research in these repositories". When people now search for a certain topic, visibility is increased.

Through CBHE projects, new Master's programmes have been initiated such as intellectual property, forensic computing and cyber-crimes which Palestine used to lack. Those joint Master's programmes have been the result of the cultural interaction between the Palestinian and European universities. Moreover, this interaction has helped in developing new international academic scholarships and programme opportunities and strengthening and sustaining the current programmes through increasing the value and the volume of international joint agreements. MS in Cyber Physical is a new topic to be introduced in Palestine. It is involved in internet big data. The objective of the project is to establish a Master project in cyber physical system which is internet of things, data minoring, big data and control systems. So, it is building an engineering system which relies on artificial intelligence. It involves partners from Palestine, Jordan, Tunisia and Europe. So, this national, regional and international interaction results in developing the curriculum syllabus, developing case studies and building a lab for cyber physical system. The researcher asked the coordinator of this project at A l-Quds University, Dr. Rashed Jayousi, if this project is sustainable and how he can measure and confirm its sustainability. He said: "it is sustainable because once we establish the degree and get the program running, surely, it will be a sustainable one because it will attract many students as it is a new technology". The coordinator added that this collaboration and cooperation extends for future plans. There is a potential of good joint research between Palestinian universities, German, British and Sweden ones since they have a research group specialized in this field. Moreover, Dr. Jayousi added that in the implementation of the cyber Master degree, there will be a joint supervision of the Master thesis, online lectures during the implementation and jointly different courses. This will maintain sustainability, cooperation and strengthen the network. Moreover, this project has paved the way to a new project that is proposed to Erasmus+ and named AgriGit. It has to do with agriculture. The results are still to be announced. If this call wins, then, a continuation of networking with the European universities and other partners prevails.

Some CBHE projects integrate with a company from the labor market to change the courses syllabi and ameliorate the courses to fit the labor market needs and exceed in employment rate.

These companies train students on mastering specific skills that bridge the gap between academia and the labor market needs. In brief, the international intervention and collaboration represented in Erasmus+ projects with the Palestinian universities through potential synergies has upgraded the Palestinian universities' profile. It has also built the capacities and competencies of the individuals by bringing the best practices to elevate the institutions in Palestine.

The Impact of Cultural Interaction at the National Level:

ICM mobility conveys culture and knowledge through interacting with other cultures either by employability or contacting with European classmates. Incoming students also add value to Palestinian universities since they share their experiences with their Palestinian classmates which eventually upgrades the whole community's thinking and behaviors. It also raises the awareness about the academic and political situation in Palestine. New horizons are opened and society accepts all transferred knowledge that endorses critical thinking which adds value to the quality of products and, therefore, ensures sustainability. ICM contributes to the modernization of higher education in different fields and the enhancement of the alumni employments. Erasmus+ ICM has also enabled cooperation and transnational exchange of experiences enhancing internationalization and competitiveness among Palestinian university staff. The exchange of experience and mobility has lifted up the capacity of stakeholders; staff, students and the whole community. High competency students who have been involved in research projects elevate the rank of their universities and are suitable for the labor market in the area of research management. Due to the experience they acquired, they run other projects.

For example, Bethlehem University shares expertise and experience at the national level through their role in METHODs project and other projects. They have sent staff to different European countries who, afterwards, have transferred and transformed the obtained skills to their home institution. Moreover, these skills are disseminated to the whole Palestinian community of higher education to assure they receive the best practice.

The development of any university in Palestine leads to the development of other universities through building capacities. During Erasmus+ projects, best practices emerge through the challenges encountered while executing these European-Palestinian projects. They lead to modified rules, standards and procedures that the Ministry of Higher Education and Scientific Research is in charge of. The Ministry of Higher Education and Scientific Research plays an integral role in the development of the Palestinian educational system through knowledge transfer and networking with the European universities. The Ministry of Higher Education and Scientific Research is sometimes a partner in some CBHE projects. This integration enables the Ministry to foster the competencies and capabilities of its staff, and improves management, governance and administrative level of the employees. Governance can be improved by adapting new international studies such as dual system, double degree system, and joint Master degrees in the majority of the high required fields. The Palestinian Ministry of Higher Education and Scientific Research has relationships and cooperation with its counterparts in Europe, the thing that elevates the quality of the Palestinian universities. The CBHE projects have elevated the Palestinian universities' profile by establishing new fields of Bachelor's, Master's and PhD level. The researcher has asked the director of Erasmus+, Dr. Nedal Jayousi, in an interview, if Erasmus+ projects play a role in elevating the QS ranking of the Palestinian universities. He said:

> Yes, Erasmus+ projects upgrade the Palestinian capacity building and it is reflected on the ranking. This is mainly due to initiating new programs that our universities do not have. Most of the funding of CBHE projects went to these

programs and it really enhances the capacity of staff institutions. It is also reflected in the ranking of our universities such as An-Najah, Birzeit and other universities.

Therefore, the interview with the director of Erasmus+ shows how the role of Erasmus+ is crucial in elevating universities' ranking, and it is a tangible one.

The Palestinian society's trust in Palestinian universities has increased since, with Erasmus+ projects implemented in these national universities, an outside stakeholder including enterprises is linked to the higher education sector, the thing that bridges the gap between academia and the labor market needs. Moreover, European experts are brought to Palestinian universities based on the needs of the universities. These experts are value adding since they seek to upgrade Palestinian universities to reach global universities' standards. Erasmus+ projects promote the concept of lifelong learning since it is a sustainable one and benefits the whole Palestinian nation. In an interview, the researcher asked the director of Erasmus+ what is meant by saying that Erasmus+ promotes lifelong learning. He said:

> One of the main aims of Erasmus+ is to ensure that there is a lifelong learning process of its CBHE projects. In fact, we have a project called lifelong learning which offers tools to ensure continuity of learning and give them access to different systems of teaching and so on. It addresses different themes. So it is one of our goals and we try to ensure that most of our projects are continuing and have continuous learning process. This is one of our strategies and it is sustainable in most of our projects.

By enrolling in Erasmus+ projects, the Palestinian universities aim at expanding any project to be at a national level. For instance, ROMOR project aims at upgrading the project to meet the requirements of the new generation of digital content repositories and integrate with other national, regional and international research repositories. Dr. Rawia, the coordinator of ROMOR project, said during an interview done by the researcher: "We are planning to build a national repository for all the Palestinian universities".

Moreover, Tefl-ePal project aims at developing the courses using the blended learning approach. What is meant by that is the development of the courses with the integration of electronic modules. This project has a national impact. It strengthens the relationship among the Palestinians universities by unifying the e-language curricula taught at the Palestinian universities and enhances collaboration and cooperation at a national level. It receives financial funds for capacity building of local universities. The researcher has interviewed Dr. Aida Bakeer, the coordinator of Tefl-ePal CBHE project, and has asked her if there is any future communication with the EU institutions. Dr. Bakeer has replied: "We have intentions for future collaboration and in fact Al-Ahliya University has signed a contract with one of the EU institutions for student exchange."

A study conducted by the project team of the European Commission and the European Union (2019) coincides with this sub-question. They both intersect in showing how the European cooperation represented by the Erasmus+ ICM and CBHE projects has an impact on the individual and the institution as well. For instance, at the individual level, they are both similar in that Erasmus+ projects seek to improve the intercultural competent skills, the entrepreneurship and innovative skills of both students and staff who are involved in the project activities. They are also taught new pedagogical skills that benefit the graduates to encounter their professional life without facing any gaps. Moreover, both the study and the sub-question emphasize on the cooperation between the higher education institutions, students and enterprise to facilitate the students' future business life. At the institutional level, on the other hand, the majority of institutions participating in Erasmus+ projects are internationally oriented due to the mutual cooperation through working together in these projects. This has resulted in renovating the curricula and pedagogical skills and adapting new tools of teaching and learning activities. METHODs project corresponds to this statement. It is built upon adapting new tools of teaching and learning such as new modalities. Erasmus+ projects play a crucial role in strengthening the participants' relations beyond any project partnership due to any sustainable cooperation. The study intersects with this sub-question in showing that Erasmus+ projects disseminate international knowledge to different types of organization. The outcome of Erasmus+ projects has led to the improvement of universities' profile, the thing that has increased the chance of student mobility and expanded the capacity of institutions to use innovative tools

4.4 Conclusion

The researcher, in this chapter, has presented the results of the main question and the sub-questions of the study with their analysis. The results have shown that Erasmus+ projects have succeeded in enabling Palestinian universities to adopt new methodologies, techniques, and educational programmes in Bachelor's, Master's, and PhD programmes through the excessive workshops, seminars, trainings, continuous CBHE projects, and the involvement of different stakeholders from the HEIs, NGOs, and other associations including mainly the Ministry of Higher Education and Scientific Research in some of CBHE projects as a partner. The role of the Ministry of Higher Education and Scientific Research improves the governance and management of the Palestinian universities. Therefore, Erasmus+, as a mechanism, enhances or has a tangible effect on enhancing intercultural communication between Palestine and the regional countries in Europe and the Middle East.

It has been observed that the sample taken from the Palestinian universities has implemented EACEA's indicators while joining Erasmus+ CBHE projects. The researcher has also remarked that these results came out from organized, well-managed projects that are built upon communication, cooperation and integration.

Moreover, each partner has his/ her own role to perform, yet they communicate together to benefit from each other's experiences. Furthermore, this inter-relation among them confirms solidarity and enables them to produce a successful and sustainable project that leads to more intercultural and international future projects. Wherefore, Erasmus+ organization and dissemination of work packages reflects these successful projects. Some of these projects are METHODS, TAP, PENs, uniGOV, MS@CPS, Tefl-ePal and ROMOR. These projects are amplified in details in the appendices section. This systematic organization that distinguishes Erasmus+ from other funding programs has proven to the researcher that through cooperation and communication, an individual can produce and function better in society. Moreover, through collaborative members, society becomes more active and productive.

Chapter five

Conclusions and Recommendations

Chapter Five

Conclusions and Recommendations

5.1 Preview

This chapter displays the conclusions and recommendations of the research, concomitant with suggestions for future researches so as to improve the quality of education and projects related to the academic field.

5.2 Conclusions

This research investigates the Erasmus+ higher education aid impact on enhancing intercultural communication in Palestine. It also assesses the quality of higher education institutions by describing the intercultural communication and cooperation that emerges among Palestine, the regional countries in Europe and the Middle East. Moreover, through the use of qualitative content analysis approach, EACEA's template forms, purposeful sampling of Erasmus+ projects conducted from 2015-2019, and based on semi-structured standardized interviews, the researcher inspects the extent of Erasmus+ impact in helping in cooperation and intercultural communication. The researcher also investigates the impact of the Erasmus + projects in bridging the socio-cultural gap between the higher education system in the Palestinian and the European institutions, and the projects' contribution in promoting the cultural knowledge between Palestine and Europe and yielding sustainable cooperation. Finally, the researcher measures the impact of cultural interaction among the higher education institutions at the individual, institutional and national level.

Erasmus+ programme is the biggest mechanism in funding higher education institutions in Palestine and elsewhere. Therefore, through the collected and analyzed results, the researcher states the following conclusions at three levels: the individual level, the institutional level and the national level.

1. Individual personal traits were developed.
2. Individuals adopted intercultural competent skills, entrepreneurship and innovative skills.
3. Adopted skills were transferred to Palestinian universities.
4. Marginalized students are considered priority at the Palestinian universities.
5. Graduates worked at the Ministry of Higher Education and Scientific Research after the termination of their studies.
6. Joint research emerged among Palestinian universities.
7. Integrated interdisciplinary research projects were elicited among university faculties such as health informatics.
8. The university- enterprise linkage bridged the socio-economic gap and accelerated employability rate.
9. The governance of the universities was improved due to the involvement of the Ministry of Higher Education and Scientific Research the thing that increased academic programmes such as: New dual system, double system and joint Master degrees.
10. New unexpected outcomes emerged from CBHE projects.
11. New Master programmes were established in Palestine for the first time such as: intellectual property, forensic computing and cyber-crimes.
12. New innovative education programmes were initiated at the Bachelor's, Master's and PhD levels.

13. New modules and best practices were adapted in Palestinian universities such as: PBL, Flipped-Classrooms and MOOCs.
14. E-port, IT centers, repositories and industry liaisons offices (ILOS) were implemented at the Palestinian universities.
15. Digital and modern learning methods were implemented.
16. The e-learning initiative bridged the educational and socio-political gaps.
17. The private sector is considered, for the first time, as a part in developing the universities curricula to meet labor market needs.
18. New laboratory facilities were established.

Moreover, it is worth mentioning that the adaptation of the European best practices and Erasmus+ synergies with Palestinian universities increased the trust in Palestinian universities that are involved in Erasmus+ projects; therefore, this elevated the Palestinian universities in QS ranking. In addition, the Erasmus+ international, national and /or regional cooperation enhanced strongly and to a large extent the Palestinian intercultural communication that promoted cultural knowledge and cultural interaction and bridged the socio-cultural gaps among Palestinian universities. As a result, this yielded sustainable and lifelong learning process through the unexpected outcomes that emerged from Erasmus+ CBHE projects. Furthermore, employment rate increased during the Erasmus+ enrollment.

Additionally, the Erasmus+ activities that where launched in Palestine were fruitful and resulted in the 50 CBHE projects with a budget of 44 million euros from (2007 - 2019). Moreover, there are 5 million euros for 150 ICM project from (2015-2019). Furthermore, Palestine, represented by the National Erasmus Office, has been granted to be project coordinators for 19 projects.

Wherefore, the success of Erasmus+ programme in Palestine is primarily due to the efforts and endeavors of the National Erasmus Office in Palestine and the Palestinian Ministry of Higher Education and Scientific Research (PICA) and the interest of the Higher Education Institutions (HEIs). Their continuous supervision and dedication to implement Erasmus+ conditions led to sustainable projects that also led to the acceleration in the employment rate in Palestine. The National Erasmus Office in Palestine and the Palestinian Ministry of Higher Education and Scientific Research (PICA) made sure that this enormous programme, with the cooperation and integration of the Palestinian universities, is implemented in Gaza and the West Bank to serve Palestinian people.

5.3 Recommendations

The researcher has the following recommendations:

Recommendations to the European Union and EACEA

1. To invest more in Erasmus+ and to build the capacities of the school system, particularly the Palestinian schools.
2. To upgrade the ICM mobility from the current duration (a semester or two) to be a degree based for two to three years so as to give sufficient time for adaptation and best practices mastering.
3. To renew the Erasmus Mundus mechanism, through Erasmus+ programme, by maximizing the fund and by building the capacity to have joint Master and double degree programmes so as to enhance the quality of education.
4. To let the European Union, intervene and facilitate travel and visa measures, particularly for Gazan students to encourage them to mobilize more.

Recommendations to National Erasmus Office in Palestine

1. To increase the ICM participation
2. To have an intensive ICM orientation day that includes videos, pamphlets and social media propagation on life in the targeted programme country in every enrolled Palestinian university in order to enlarge the circle of participants and reduce the vagueness that evolves around the recipient country.
3. To increase the involvement of enterprise at the Palestinian universities to encompass all faculties such as arts and humanities, for example: to involve translation centers to train English and translation major students to qualify them to master the basics of translation in order to be ready as freelancers.

Recommendations to the Ministry of Higher Education and Scientific Research and the Palestinian Universities

1. To increase the participation of the Ministry of Higher Education and Scientific Research in Erasmus+ CBHE projects as a partner in order to foster the projects results and apply them to other educational institutions within the same field.
2. To adopt more new educational programmes to be implemented at the Palestinian universities.
3. To have clear policies of higher education and strategic plan.
4. To facilitate the accreditation of the new educational programmes funded by Erasmus+.
5. To have the Higher Education Reform Experts (HEREs) set a monthly meeting with the project coordinators to keep updated with the projects progress.

6. To strengthen the relationship between the Ministry of Higher Education and Scientific Researrch and the project coordinators, thus, to ensure communication with the Ministry to abide by its rules and procedures.
7. Students should be exposed at an early age to the notion of thinking internationally, so as when they reach university level, they can be easily hooked to any youth mobility communication.
8. Universities should prepare their students to study abroad by increasing the number of incoming professors and students from international countries to bridge the socio-cultural gaps and encourage the cultural interaction among them.
9. Staff, represented by professors, should encourage students to break their fear barrier and engage in Erasmus+ exchange mobility.
10. Erasmus+ units should be available at every Palestinian university in order to be ready for all student's inquiries.

5.4 Suggestions for Scholars to Further Studies

1. To conduct more researches about Erasmus+ CBHE projects in Palestine and provide free access to them and this is due to the scarcity of researches on this domain.
2. To conduct more researches on Erasmus+ ICM mobility in Palestine and make them easily and freely accessible to all due to lack of local studies on this domain.
3. To have a comparative study between Erasmus+ programme and other educational programmes to see how they can enhance and benefit each other, and thus, develop education in Palestine.
4. Finally, to have a follow-up study to this study by using the quantitative approach alongside the current qualitative one in order to have an in-depth description of the Palestinian intercultural communication.

5. To have a national database of Erasmus and similar projects.

References

AQAC Palestine. (2020). Retrieved March 11, 2020 from Ministry of Higher Education: http://www.aqac.mohe.gov.ps/en/

Austrian Institute of Technology (AIT), Directorate-General for Education, Youth, Sport and Culture (European Commission), Public Policy and Management Institute (PPMI). (2019, 05 17). Study on the impact of Erasmus+ higher education partnerships and knowledge alliances at local, national and European levels on key higher education policy priorities. European Union, Publication Office. Luxembourg: European Union. Retrieved from European Commission.

Berchin, I. I., Sima, M., de Lima, M. A., Biesel, S., dos Santos, L. P., Ferreira, R. V., ... & Ceci, F. (2018). The importance of international conferences on sustainable development as higher education institutions' strategies to promote sustainability: A case study in Brazil. *Journal of cleaner production*, 171, 756-772.

Birzeit University. (2019, January 30). An Erasmus experience of a lifetime: exchange student shares her journey at BZU. Retrieved February 17, 2020 from Birzeit University: https://www.birzeit.edu/en/blogs/erasmus-experience-lifetime-exchange-student-shares-her-journey-bzu?fbclid=IwAR1kZs4mvSQOPdNQjBMS4np

Bryła, P. (2015). The impact of international student mobility on subsequent employment and professional career: A large-scale survey among Polish former Erasmus students. *Procedia-Social and Behavioral Sciences*, 176, 633-641.

Chevening Scholarship. (2019). Retrieved October 12, 2019, from https://www.chevening.org/scholarship/occupied-palestinian-territories/.

Cinotti, A., Ferrari, L., Righini, G., & Emili, E. A. (2018). The MUSE project. Improving access, participation and learning of students with disability in Latin American universities1.

Ckeshek. (2020, February 24). Faculty of Business and Economics forges long-term collaborations with three companies. Retrieved March 3, 2020, from https://www.birzeit.edu/ar/node/42642

Clemente-Ricolfe, J. S., & García-Pinto, P. (2019). Erasmus University Students Motivation and Segments: The Case of Universitat Politècnica de València, Spain. *Journal of Educational and Social Research*, 9(2), 72.

Commission, E. (Version 3.0 – December 2018). Erasmus+ International Credit Mobility. In E. Commission, *Handbook for Participating Organizations*. European Commission.

Cunningham, P. (2019). International credit mobility [PowerPoint slides]. Retrieved November 20, 2019, from https://slideplayer.com/slide/14802077/?fbclid=IwAR3rSO5jkCxSywqRUTfh9hoAMNUcmm8DWcKv4HnLDYAV_WRZf4kywBQMn_I

DAAD. (2019.). Retrieved September 22, 2019, from https://www.daad-eastjerusalem.org/en/about-us/about-the-daad/.

European Commission. (2019). Erasmus Mundus Programme. Retrieved October 10, 2019, from EACEA: https://eacea.ec.europa.eu/sites/2007-2013/erasmus-mundus-programme_en

European Commission. (2019). Tempus Programme. Retrieved October 14, 2019, from EACEA: https://eacea.ec.europa.eu/sites/2007-2013/tempus-programme_en

European Commission (2018). In Erasmus+, *Handbook for Participating Organizations* (p. 7).

Education Development Program. (2014, July 21). Retrieved September 22, 2019, from https://www.usaid.gov/west-bank-and-gaza/fact-sheets/education-development-program-jan-2014.

Education, Training and Youth. (2019, April 12). Retrieved September 8, 2019, from European Union: https://europa.eu/european-union/topics/education-training-youth_en

Enfield, S. (2019). Evidence for soft power created via scholarship schemes. Occupied Palestinian Territories (Chevening Scholarship). (2019.). Retrieved September 15, 2019, from https://www.chevening.org/scholarship/occupied-palestinian-territories/.

Erasmus+. (2019). creating opportunities for the UK across Europe. Retrieved November 18, 2019, from participating countries: https://www.erasmusplus.org.uk/participating-countries#Programme%20Countries

Erasmus+ Programme. (2019). Key Action 1: Learning Mobility of Individuals. Retrieved September 6, 2019, from National Erasmus Office in Palestine: https://www.erasmusplus.ps/page-804-en.html

European Commission. (2015, April 29). News EU Budget. Retrieved January 7, 2020, from Budget: https://ec.europa.eu/budget/news/article_en.cfm?id=201504291534

European Union. (2019). CBHE Results 2019. Retrieved September 11, 2019, from National Erasmus Office in Palestine: https://www.erasmusplus.ps/page-814-en.html

European Union. (2019). Jean Monnet. Retrieved September 15, 2019 from EACEA: https://eacea.ec.europa.eu/erasmus-plus/actions/jean-monnet_en

Fulbright Foreign Student Program. (2019, December 24). Retrieved September 28, 2019, from https://www.amideast.org/west-bank-gaza/find-a-scholarship/graduate-study/fulbright-foreign-student-program

Haj-Yehia, K., & Erez, M. (2018, September). The impact of the ERASMUS program on cultural identity: A case study of an Arab Muslim female student from Israel. *In Women's Studies International Forum* (Vol. 70, pp. 32-38).

Heyneman, S. P., & Lee, B. (2016). International organizations and the future of education assistance. *International Journal of Educational Development*, 48, 9-22.

Higher Education Scholarship Palestine (HESPAL). (2019.). Retrieved October 2, 2019,from https://www.britishcouncil.ps/en/study-uk/scholarships/hespal.

Ho, H. F., Lin, M. H., & Yang, C. C. (2015). Goals, Strategies, and Achievements in the Internationalization of Higher Education in Japan and Taiwan. *International Education Studies,* 8(3), 55-65.

icmhandbook. (2018). In international credit mobility budget (p. 9).

international credit mobility budget. (2018). In international credit mobility (p. 9).

Jovanovska, M. B., Neshkovska, S., Trajkovska, D. A., Tabakovska, N. B., & KuzmanovskaTasetovikj, B. (2018). University Students' Views on the Impact of Student Mobility on their Achievements and Future Prospects. *Journal of Contemporary Educational Studies*/Sodobna Pedagogika, 69(2).

Marktanner, M., & Merkel, A. (2019). Conflict and aid dependency–an explorative study motivated by the case of Palestine. *Journal of Development Effectiveness*, 1-20.

Mense, E. G., Lemoine, P. A., Garretson, C. J., & Richardson, M. D. (2018). The Development of Global Higher Education in a World of Transformation. *Journal of Education and Development*, 2(3), 47.

Ministry of Higher Education and Palestinian Scientific Research. (2019). moehe creation. Retrieved September 26, 2019, from Ministry of Higher Education and Scientific Research: http://www.mohe.pna.ps/moehe/plansandstrategies

Ministry of Higher Education and Scientific Research. (2019). Vision and Mission. Retrieved September 28, 2019, from Ministry of Higher Education and Scientific Research: http://www.mohe.pna.ps/moehe/visionandmission

N. A. (2019). Mobility, Erasmus+ International Credit: Handbook for Participating Organizations. European Commission.

National Erasmus Office in Palestine. (2019, February 6). The Islamic University of Gaza. Retrieved September 9, 2019,from Facebook: https://www.facebook.com/watch/?v=389191054974084

National Erasmus Office in Palestine. (2019). Actions. Retrieved October 17, 2019,from Erasmus=: https://www.erasmusplus.ps/page-581-en.html

National Erasmus Office in Palestine. (2019, July). International Credit Mobility 2018. Retrieved January 11,2020, from Newsletter: http://eurireland.ie/assets/uploads/2019/08/NEO-PS-Newsletter-July-2019.pdf

National Erasmus Office in Palestine . (2019, February 6). The Islamic University of Gaza. Retrieved December 21,2019 from Facebook: https://www.facebook.com/watch/?v=389191054974084

ÖNEN, S. (2017). AN INVESTIGATION INTO THE EXPERIENCES OF ERASMUS STUDENTS. *Journal of Hasan Ali Yücel Faculty of Education/Hasan Ali Yücel Egitim Fakültesi Dergisi (HAYEF),* 14(1).

Patton, M. Q. (1990). *Qualitative evaluation and research methods*. SAGE Publications, Inc.

Penprase, B. E. (2018). The fourth industrial revolution and higher education. *In Higher education in the era of the fourth industrial revolution* (pp. 207-229). Palgrave Macmillan, Singapore.

Perna, L. W., Orosz, K., Gopaul, B., Jumakulov, Z., Ashirbekov, A., & Kishkentayeva, M. (2014). Promoting human capital development: A typology of international scholarship programs in higher education. *Educational Researcher*, 44(2), 63-73.

Pergamon. Maldonado-Mahauad, J., Hilliger, I., De Laet, T., Millecamp, M., Verbert, K., Ochoa, X., & Pérez-Sanagustín, M. (2018). The LALA Project: Building Capacity to Use Learning Analytics to Improve Higher Education in Latin America. *In companion proceedings of the 8th international learning analytics & knowledge conference* (pp. 630-637)

Power, C. (2014). *The power of education: Education for all, development, globalization and UNESCO* (Vol. 27). Springer.

programme, E. (2019). Key Action 1: Learning Mobility of Individuals. Retrieved November 25,2019 from National Erasmus Office in Palestine: https://www.erasmusplus.ps/page-585-en.html

programme, E. (2019). Ahmad Albuhaisi- ICM Student. Retrieved from National Erasmus Office in Palestine.

Purpose, Content and History of Jean Monnet Scholarship Programme. (2019.). Retrieved October 5,2019 from Jean Monnet: https://www.jeanmonnet.org.tr/en/About-Us/About-Scholarship-Programme

Rantisi, E., & Saleh, M. (2015). evaluating the scholarships managed by the British council in Palestine on the leadership capacity building of the alumni. evaluating the scholarships managed by the British council in Palestine on the leadership capacity building of the alumni.

Ruptly. [YouTube]. (2019, May 4). State of Palestine: Italian trainee doctor becomes first-ever Erasmus student in Gaza [Video file]. Retrieved from

Safi, D. (2012). Retrieved October 16,2019 from http://www.care-palestine.com/tempus-project.html

Silva, P., Nogueiro, T., Saraiva, M., Jorge, F., Radzeviciene, A., & Chuong, T. (2018). A Capacity Building for Higher Education ERASMUS+ Project: Strategic Human Resources Management for Southeast Asian Universities (HR4ASIA). *Silva.*

Souto-Otero, M. (2019). Erasmus+ Higher Education Impact Study. Brussels: European Commission.

Törnberg, P., & Törnberg, A. (2019). Laying the foundations for a relational mixed methods social network analysis. *Mixed Methods Social Network Analysis: Theories and Methodologies in Learning and Education*, 6.

Union, E. (2019). Education, Training and Youth. Retrieved September 20, 2019 from European Union: https://europa.eu/european-union/topics/education-training-youth_en

United Nations conference on TRADE AND DEVELOPMENT. (2019, September 10). Palestinian Socioeconomic crises now at breaking point. Retrieved November 4, 2019, from United Nations conference on TRADE AND DEVELOPMENT: https://unctad.org/en/pages/newsdetails.aspx?OriginalVersionID=2180

University, B. (2019, January 30). An Erasmus experience of a lifetime: exchange student shares her journey at BZU. Retrieved from Birzeit University: https://www.birzeit.edu/en/blogs/erasmus-experience-lifetime-exchange-student-shares-her-journey-bzu?fbclid=IwAR1kZs4mvSQOPdNQjBMS4npF1btnO_ecIgd48XV5j_tOzkWzGC4XaYLDwZU

Vaismoradi, M., Jones, J., Turunen, H., & Snelgrove, S. (2016). Theme development in qualitative content analysis and thematic analysis. *Journal of Nursing Education and Practice. (Vol. 6), No 5.*

VERHOEVEN, J. (2019). 14. UNDERSTANDING HIGHER EDUCATION SYSTEM REFORM. *Higher Education System Reform: An International Comparison after Twenty Years of Bologna,* 221.

World Bank. (2017, October 05). higher education. Retrieved October 11,2019, from The world bank: https://www.worldbank.org/en/topic/tertiaryeducation

World Bank. (2019, October 15). Education overview. Retrieved October 12, 2019, from The world bank: https://www.worldbank.org/en/topic/education/overview#4

Zamala university fellowship program. (2018, May 30). Retrieved June 06, 2020, from https://www.taawon.org/en/media/news/zamala-university-fellowship-program

.

Appendices

Appendix (A) CBHE projects Summaries

561940-EPP-1-2015-1-JO-EPPKA2-CBHE-JP METHODS- Modernization of teaching methodologies in higher education: EU experience for Jordan and Palestinian territory

Project summary

The project aims at improving the quality of teaching and learning at the PC universities through incorporating technological tools in consistence with pedagogical best practices and by building the capacity of the universities to evaluate, develop and design e-curricula to be available on an open accessible portal. To achieve this objective, the project will support establishing a national Center in both Jordan (in JU) and Palestine (in BZU) to be as a hub for utilizing best practices in ICT in education in both PCs . These Centers will facilitate establishing diverse clusters (pool of staff members from target discipline in Engineering and science faculty with multimedia and educational specialists interested in a certain discipline) from PC universities where an educational specialists will review the proposed learning material in order to ensure compatibility with the standards; and multimedia designers who will design the interfaces, activities, presentation, layout and animation included in the e-curricula.

Project objectives

The aim of METHODS project is to raise the competencies of individual learners to become active members of the knowledge society by enhancing the learning process of students acquiring 21st Century competencies to become autonomous and active learners

The Objectives:

- Training and follow up with lecturers/professors on how to develop, share learning objects, and collaborate their e-courses on the portal.
- Establish a well-equipped national center in both Jordan and Palestine interested in modernizing higher education and moving toward knowledge-based economy.
- Create a hub of competences aims to improve quality of teaching and learning by building the capacity of the PC universities how to evaluate, develop and design e-curricula.
- Enhance the cooperation with EU partners through mutual visits to develop strategies how to move from teaching to learning and develop scalable sustainable solutions.
- Create a pool of experts and clusters of targeted disciplines (Engineering and science) in this area

Project consortium

- Birzeit University, PS
- An-Najah National University, PS
- Bethlehem University, PS
- Palestine Polytechnic University,PS
- The University of Jordan, JO
- The Hashemite University, JO
- Jordan University of Science and Technology, JO
- Al-Zaytoonah University of Jordan, JO
- University of Wolverhampton, UK
- Leipzig University of Applied Sciences,
- University of Deusto, ES
- Plovdiv University, BG
- Universitat de Girona
- Aalborg University Copenhagen, DK
- World University Service, ES

Budget
990 590,00 €

Duration
36 months

Reference: 586301-EPP-1-2017-1-PS-EPPKA2-CBHE-JP Pathway in Enterprise Systems Engineering

DESCRIPTION:

The PENS project seeks to build capacities to develop a new curricula in enterprise systems engineering as a new undergraduate program, using a student centred adaptive learning approach based on the bologna processes. The project will develop 8 courses in total and four tutorials. Also it promote entrepreneurship education. These new Pathway in Enterprise systems engineering will be deployed at the four participating partner universities, two in Palestine (P4: AQU, P5:BZU) and two in Tunisia (P7:US, P8:UM). The uniqueness of this approach, that to meet the multidisciplinary needs of the two domains (engineering and system thinking), it will develop an innovative user-centred adaptive learning to create a new

curricula and enable the four universities to implement developed program within their degrees addressing variations, yet meeting their own specified key learning outcomes.

The importance of enterprise systems engineering to be part of the undergraduate training as integral part of their educational skills, is critical to advance the ICT sector towards evidence-based practices, in the region, which is currently

developing. These skills are essential to solidify the deeper understanding of the value and importance of enterprise engineering not only to their specialty, but also their profession, work and practice. They will promote the uptake and implementation of enterprise system engineering to become essential part of their profession as enabling mechanisms to improve the quality of ICT. Thus one key objective of PENS is to develop capacity of members of faculty in enterprise systems engineering and create undergraduate program to ensure sustainability and lasting impact.

Coordinator: THE BOARD OF TRUSTEES OF THE BIR ZEIT UNIVERSITY
AL MARJ STREET 1
BIRZEIT 627,PS
Phone : +97022982916
Email : yhassouneh@birzeit.edu
Internet site address :
Contact: Dr. Yousef Hassouneh

Partners:

Al-Andalus Software Development and Technology (I.C.D) ,PS
Al-Quds University ,PS
Middlesex University Higher Education

Corporation ,UK
Proxym IT ,TN
Universidad De Alcala ,ES
Universita Delgi Studi Di Cagliari ,IT
University Of Monastir ,TN
University of Sousse ,TN

Application Grant Requested 972,899
Contract Duration: 36 months

REFERENCE: 598405-EPP-1-2018-1-PS-EPPKA2-CBHE-JP
TITLE: Teaching English as Foreign Language in Palestinian HEIs: An e-Learning Initiative that Bridges Educational and Socio-Political Gaps

Description: Freedom and participation in the academic world are crucial factors that motivated QOU to submit TEFL proposal. Palestine has been restricted inside its borders due to socio-political reasons. The occupation in Pal impacts the movement of people, divides the territory geographically and socio-politically. This has led to inequitable access to quality education for all students. Moreover, academics are struggling to communicate and interact with peers from countries all over the world, due to the language barrier. The exchange of knowledge, skills and culture with others poses as a great challenge for the Palestinian HEIs. These challenges 'built walls' prevent from being active and critical members of a growing global community.

Teaching English in Pal faces great challenges and difficulties at all levels, in all domains. MoEHE (2015), Rixon (2013), attribute the challenges to several reasons, such as poor and inappropriate content, traditional teaching methodologies, lack of professional educators in TEFL to integrate educational technology, and missing modern learning spaces; the continuing dissatisfaction with the overall performance and proficiency of students in English language (EL) is attributed to the quality of instruction affected by lack of access to technology and unappealing materials and lack of motivation TEFL-ePal aims to develop flexible curricula, with face-to-face and online courses to be accessible to all learners, with no restrictions, reaching all learners including those with special needs and conditions, learners at work & women with restrictions. It aims to implement initiatives that develop learners' linguistic capacity, skills, and English language excellence, enhance modernization, internationalization and lifelong

learning without ignoring the culture.
The innovative character of the project serves the capacity-building aspect for Palestinian HEIs and bridges the gaps, addresses inclusion and the proper technological development.

Coordinator: AL-QUDS OPEN UNIVERSITY ALERSAL STREET- KANAAN BUILDING – RAMALLAH – 0970. PS
Phone : +970-22964571/2/3/4
Email : tefl_erasmus@qou.edu
Internet site address : http://www.qou.edu

Partners:		
	AL-ISTIQLAL UNIVERSITY	PS
	ANADOLU UNIVERSITY	TR
	CONFIDENCE FOR LEARNING AND TRAININING	PS
	PALESTINE AHLIYA UNIVERSITY COLLEGE	PS
	PALESTINE TECHNICAL UNIVERSITY - KADOORIE (PTUK)	PS
	TECHNISCHE UNIVERSITAET CHEMNITZ	DE
	UNIVERSAL LEARNING SYSTEMS LTD	IE
	UNIVERSITY OF WOLVERHAMPTON	UK

Grant Requested 929,151 EUR
Project Duration 36 months

Activity Curriculum development
Region(s) Region 3 - South Mediterranean Countries

573700-EPP-1-2016-1-PS-EPPKA2-CBHE-JP Research Output Management through Open Access Institutional Repositories in Palestinian Higher Education

Project objectives

ROMOR aims to sustainably enhance the practice of research output management in the PS HEIs through enabling OAIRs as well as the advocacy in support of Open Access to research outputs. The specific objectives are:

-map the current status of research dissemination in 4 PS HEIs and to identify the needs to integrate scholarly publishing and dissemination at these universities
-prepare training and teaching material meeting the local needs for building capacity in implementing OAIR
-build capacity needed for building, managing and sustaining OAIR
-design and build 4 OAIRs in partner PS HEIs that interface with outputs such as journals, books, conference proceedings, theses, and research data
-investigate key issues in populating and maintaining collections
scale-up the IUG IR to serve as a national OAIR
-share widely the skills gained and to assist non-partner PS HEIs in setting up their OAIR
-raise the awareness and promote collaborating and sharing of experience with different non- HEI stakeholders

Project summary

The ROMOR Project aims over the course of three years to build capacity on research output management in four leading PS HEIs by establishing Open Access Institutional Repositories. The training which is required to establish these repositories, and then their implementation, population and management will be the core of the Project. Learning outcomes from these activities will also be shared and disseminated in a variety of ways, including the establishment of mechanisms to assist proactively other institutions in setting up and managing repositories.
This Project aims to improve not only the visibility and the management of scientific research, but also to support the advocacy in support of open access to research outputs and to foster scholarly communication and coordination between PS HEIs.
The Project comprises 4 PS HEIs (IUG, BZU, QOU, and KAD) and 4 EU HEIs (TUWIEN, PARMA, BU, and GLA).

Project consortium

- Islamic University of Gaza
- Al-Quds Open University
- Palestine Technical University – Kadoorie (PTUK),
- The Board of Trustees of The Birzeit University, PS
- Technische Universitaet Wien, AT
- Universita Degli Studi Di Parma IT
- University of Brighton, UK
- University of Glasgow, UK

Budget
1,117,516.00
Duration
36 months

573684-EPP-1-2016-1-PS-EPPKA2-CBHE-JP Improving Governance Practices and Palestinian Higher

Education Institutions

Project objectives

1- Create a enabling environment to adopt decent governance, management and accountability practices
2- Establish a clear governance framework, including well-defined and clear mission and goals.
2- Establish an effective governance and management structures
3- Stimulate autonomy and accountability,
4- Strengthen links with different stakeholders (i.e. improve participation) in strategic planning and development activities (this will reduce the gap between recent graduates and the industry).

Project summary

University Governance plays a crucial role in developing higher education institutions. It describes how the HEIs define goals, implement plans, assign responsibilities, take decisions, and measure achievements. University Governance is an important factor of success, not only because of its concern of goal definition and impact measurements, but also it includes the approach by which the university leadership can succeed through implementing values such as transparency, participation, accountability and autonomy. The UniGov project seeks to develop the 5 dimensions of university governance (namely: context and mission, management, autonomy, accountability, and transparency and participation) to improve the HEIs in partner countries. This can be achieved only by taking exemplar universities for the EU and developing a set of interventions (through WPs and activities) to address this issue.
Based on the communications: "Increasing the impact of EU development strategy: an agenda for change" and " European higher education in the work", this project seeks to support the modernization, accessibility, and internationalization of HEIs in Palestine, through addressing 5 cross-cutting aspects of governance.
outcomes.

Project consortium

- **An-Najah National University**
- **Arab American University**
- **Islamic University of Gaza PS**
- **Palestine Polytechnic University, PS**
- **The Board of Trustees of Birzeit University, PS**
- **Unimed Unione Delle Universita Delmedit Teraneo Associazione, IT**
- **Universidade De Evora PT**
- **Universit A' Degli Studi Di Siena, IT**
- **University College Cork – National University of Ireland, CORK, IE**
- **Univerza V LJUBLJANI, SI**

Budget
856.840,00

Duration
36 months

561651-EPP-1-2015-1-IT-EPPKA2-CBHE-JP OpenMEd- A bottom-up approach for opening up education in

South-Mediterranean countries

Project objectives

The specific objectives of the project are to:

1) Raise awareness and widen HEI participation in Open Educational Practices and Resources;

2) Define the OER Agenda for the re-use of OER at HE institutional level;

3) Define mid-term strategic roadmaps for the implementation of the OER Agenda at local-institutional level according to the local, cultural and institutional needs and strategies;

4) Teach university teachers how to use and repurpose OER in a pedagogically-rich context and improve their digital competences;

5) Pilot start-up open educational practices and offer to students flexible and up to date open contents and learning paths, with a linkage to the international community and the needs of the job market.

Project summary

The project explores the adoption of strategies and channels that embrace the principles of openness and reusability within the context of South-Mediterranean HEIs. The overall objective of OpenMEd is to widen participation and adoption of Open Educational Resources (OER) and Open Educational Practices (OEP) as a bottom-up approach to support the modernisation of HEIs in Morocco, Palestine and Egypt and Jordan, improving the quality of education and teaching. The initiative also opens the possibility to provide free educational resources for self-learners, in terms of informal and lifelong learning.

OEP are defined as practices which support the production, use and reuse of high quality Open Educational Resources through institutional policies, which promote innovative pedagogical models, and respect and empower learners as co-producers on their lifelong learning path. OEP address the whole OER governance community: policy makers, managers and administrators of organizations, educational professionals and learners. (cfr. ICDE, International Council for Open and Distance Education).

Project Consortium

- Birzeit University, PS
- An-Najah National University, PS
- UNIMED UNIONE DELLE UNIVERSITA DELMEDITTERANEO ASSOCIAZIONE
- Alexandria University, EG
- Association of Arab Universities, JO
- Cairo University, EG
- Coventry University, UK
- German Jordanian University, JO
- Politecnico Di Tornio, IT
- Princess Sumaya University for Technology, JO
- Universidad De Sevilla, ES
- Universidad Internacional De LA Rioja Sa, ES
- Universite Cadi Ayyad, MA
- Universite Ibn Zohr, MA
- European Distance And E-Learning Networking LBG, UK

Duration: 36 months

Budget

EUR 871,299.00

REFERENCE : 598750-EPP-1-2018-1-DE-EPPKA2-CBHE-JP

TITLE: INTERNATION MASTER OF SCIENCE ON CYBER PHYSICAL SYSTEMS

Description: MS@CPS is a collaborative effort among EU and MENA countries for the establishment of an International Master of Computer Systems on Cyber Physical Systems. The envisioned master programme will focus on the contemporary recent technologies in the fields of Embedded Systems (ES) and Knowledge-based Systems (KBS) that provide the needed expertise for a CPS education and tremendous economic opportunities and furthermore span various important applications in our daily life such as: Internet of Things (IoT), autonomous cars, smart phones, embedded systems, big data, semantic computing, cloud computing, etc.
The curriculum of MS@CPS program will be designed by analyzing the existing curricula in the area of embedded and knowledge-based systems, then a field study of market requirements and needs in the MENA region will be conducted. In parallel, the consortium members will review and examine pedagogical teaching and learning methods to fulfil the program objectives. Further, the curriculum of MS@CPS will be strongly aligned with the special requirements of the industry in the MENA countries in order to establish the skills of the students for strengthening the economy. In particular, MS@CPS will arrange several activities in cooperation with the industry partners to provide an open platform for students and industry, which will strengthen the students' skills and establish joint internships and master thesis. By providing solid skills in entrepreneurship and adopting proven mechanisms from program countries, the graduated students of MS@CPS will be able to establish their own start-ups.
By enrolling in this program, the students will benefit from the multi-cultural experience and contact with different teaching styles responding to labour market needs, foster innovation and create top talents as the mobility readiness and complex system solution handling are highly valued skills for technology-driven companies.

Coordinator: UNIVERSITAET SIEGEN
ADOLF REICHWEIN
STRASSE 2A SIEGEN
57076,DE
Phone : +49 271- 740 3332
Email :
roman.obermaisser@uni-
siegen.de Internet site address :

Partners:

AL-QUDS UNIVERSITY	PS
CARTHAGE UNIVERSITY	TN
GERMAN JORDANIAN UNIVERSITY	JO
KUNGLIGA TEKNISKA HOEGSKOLAN	SE
PALESTINE TECHNICAL COLLEGE -DEIR ELBALAH	PS
SFAX UNIVERSITY	TN
TAFILA TECHNICAL UNIVERSITY	JO
THE UNIVERSITY OF HERTFORDSHIRE HIGHER EDUCATION CORPORATION	U

Grant Requested 999,976.18 EUR
Project Duration 36 months

Activity Curriculum development
Region(s) Region 3 - South Mediterranean Countries

573738-EPP-1-2016-1-PS-EPPKA2-CBHE-SP Transforming Assessment Practices in Large Enrollment First Year Education

Project objectives

• allowing for time-efficient assessment and feedback practices
• providing learners with self-learning opportunities
• engaging learners in giving feedback to their own peers
• improving the quality of interaction in large group instructions
• developing innovative technology supported classroom assessment techniques
• creating better match between freshman skills and market requirements in professional degree programs
• providing timely feedback and satisfaction rate on large group ins

Project summary

The proposed project will address a three-fold problem in the Palestinian higher education. It targets: a) the theoretically and content-based freshman instruction and assessment, b) the absence of formative assessment and self-directed learning at this transitional stage, and c) the lack or complete absence of technology supported assessment modules in large group instruction.
Technology offers a wide range of options for self-regulated learning and for providing teachers with timely feedback on learner achievements and on their satisfaction with the materials and the learning strategies.
Therefore, this project will use available technology options to provide timely feedback for learners and teachers in the context of massive education so improvement and adjustment strategies can be done on time.
The outcome-based assessment in freshman education and adopting technology supported self-directed learning activities will help mitigate the negative impacts these problems may have on the quality of higher education country wide.
outcomes.

Project consortium

- An-Najah National University
- Accreditation and Quality Assurance Commission
- Alaqsa University PS
- Palestine Polytechnic University
- The board of Trustees of the Birzeit University
- University College of Applied Sciences
- Astik imt Kerdoskopiki Etaireia Kaimi Kubernitiki Organosi Four Elements, EL
- Slovenska Technicka Univerzita V Bratislave, SK
- Universidad De Alicante, ES
- University College Cork – National University of Ireland, Cork, IE

Budget
508.118,00
Duration
36 months

Appendix (B) list of interviews

Name of the interviewees	Institution	Date and Time of the interview	Positions	CBHE project	Questions of the interviews
Dr. Muhammad Najjar	An-Najah National University-Palestine	March,15, 2020 At 10:00 AM	Director of Project Management and Consulting Unit (PMCU)	The coordinator of uniGOV CBHE Project	• To give a synopsis of their projects • If the project is sustainable and if yes, how sustainability of the project is measured.
Dr. Wasel Ghanem	Birzeit University	March, 15, 2020 At 12:00 AM	Assistant Professor Faculty Member-Department of Electrical and Computer Engineering	The coordinator of METHODS CBHE Project	• To see if there are any unexpected outcomes and any new intercultural communication between Palestinian HEIs and the European Union.

Dr. Aida Bakeer	Al-Quds Open University	March, 16, 2020 At 3:00 PM	Assistant Professor in Faculty of Education and Educational Sciences	The coordinator of TEFL-ePAL
Dr.Rawia Awadallah	The Islamic University of Gaza (IUG)	March 16, 2020 At 5:00 PM	Vice Dean of Scientific Research, Assistant Professor of Computer Science	The coordinator of ROMOR CBHE Project
Dr. Abdel Karim Daraghmeh	An-Najah National University	March 18, 2020 At 1:00 PM	Director of the Center of Excellence in Teaching and Learning	The coordinator of TAP CBHE Project
Dr. Yousef Hassouneh	Birzeit University	March 19, 2020 At 11:30 AM	Assistant Professor Faculty Member - Department of Computer Science	The coordinator of PENS

				CBHE Project
Dr. Rashid Jayousi	Al-Quds University Abu- Deis	March 19, 2020 At 4:00 PM	Assistant Professor at CS and IT department Computer Science Department	The coordinator of MS@CPS CBHE Project

الملخص

يتميز برنامج إيراسموس+ بأنه ذو الية كبيرة في تمويل مؤسسات التعليم العالي في فلسطين ودول أخرى في مختلف المناطق وهو برنامج ممول من قبل الاتحاد الأوروبي ويقوم بدعم الأفراد والمؤسسات على حد سواء. عمل برنامج ايراسموس+ على تحديث وابتكار وتجديد نظم التعليم العالي بميزانية تعادل ١٦,٥ بليون يورو. من ناحية أخرى، عزز برنامج ايراسموس+ حوكمة التعليم العالي وتدويله. نظرا لعدم وجود دراسات سابقه في فلسطين حول أهمية وأثر هذا البرنامج على التعليم العالي ورغم تمويله الضخم في هذا الأطار، أجرى الباحث هذه الدراسة لمعرفة أثر الدعم الدولي على المؤسسات التعليمية الفلسطينية.

الهدف من الدراسة: الهدف الرئيس من الدراسة هو معرفة أثر الدعم الدولي لبرامج التعليم العالي في تعزيز التواصل بين الثقافات وقد تناول الباحث برامج ايراسموس+ في فلسطين كحالة خاصة. واستقصى الباحث مدى تأثير برامج ايراسموس+ على التعاون والتواصل الدولي بين الثقافات. اقتفى الباحث أثر مشاريع ايراسموس+ ليرى مدى سد الفجوة الاجتماعية والثقافية بين نظم التعليم العالي في المؤسسات الفلسطينية والأوروبية. بالإضافة الى ذلك، قام الباحث بالتقصي عن أهمية دور مشاريع ايراسموس+ في تعزيز المعرفة الثقافية بين فلسطين وأوروبا ومعرفة مدى استدامة هذه المشاريع. أخيرا قام الباحث بقياس أثر التفاعل الثقافي بين مؤسسات التعليم العالي على ثلاثة مستويات وهي كما يلي: المستوى الفردي والمستوى المؤسسي والمستوى الوطني (المحلي).

التصميم/ منهجية وأداة البحث: استخدم الباحث التحليل الوصفي النوعي لانتقاء وتصنيف جميع الوثائق التي تم تجميعها من الجامعات الفلسطينية والتي تتعلق ببرامج ايراسموس+ للحراك الطلابي وبناء قدرات التعليم العالي. قام الباحث بتصنيف وتبويب الوثائق التي تصف أثر مشاريع ايراسموس+ على الجامعات الفلسطينية المشاركة في هذه المشاريع. ولذلك استخدم الباحث نموذج ايكيا (EACEA) في تجميع البيانات من الجامعات الفلسطينية والتي تصف أثر مشاريع ايراسموس على المستويات الثلاثة الفردية والمؤسساتية والوطنية.

عينة الدراسة: قام الباحث بأخذ عينات تستهدف سبعة مشاريع تابعة لايراسموس+ ذو أثر على المستويات الثلاثة وتم تنفيذها ما بين عام 2015 و2019 من قبل الجامعات الفلسطينية المستهدفة كجامعة بيرزيت، وجامعة النجاح الوطنية، وجامعة الخليل، وجامعة الأزهر، وبيت لحم، والجامعة الإسلامية، والكلية الجامعية للعلوم التطبيقية. تمثل عينة الدراسة 41% من مجموع مشاريع ايراسموس+ التي تؤول الى 50 مشروع بناء قدرات التعليم العالي وحوالي 2200 حراك طلابي بقيمة 44 مليون يورو.

النتائج: تبين بعد التحليل وعن كثب أن مشاريع ايراسموس+ لها أثر على ثلاثة مستويات وأهمها على المستوى الفردي وذلك بحيازة الخريجين على وظائف عديدة في القطاعين الحكومي وغير الحكومي بما في ذلك وزارة التعليم العالي. أما على المستوى المؤسسي، أنشأت برامج جديدة تُدرس لأول مرة في فلسطين مثل برنامج الملكية الفكرية والجرائم الإلكترونية والحوسبة الجنائية. وعلى الصعيد الوطني، أدت مشاركة وزارة التعليم العالي الجامعات في مشاريع ايراسموس+ الى تحسين إدارة هذه الجامعات وبالتالي ارتفاع أدائها. هذه النتائج تعكس بمنحى إيجابي نجاح برنامج ايراسموس+ في تعزيز التواصل بين الثقافات وذلك بين فلسطين ودول المنطقة في أوروبا والشرق الأوسط.

التوصيات: أوصى الباحث على ضرورة الاستثمار بشكل أكبر في برامج ايراسموس+ لبناء قدرات الجامعات الفلسطينية. وأوصى ايضا بضرورة توسيع نطاق برامج ايراسموس+ لتغطية جميع القطاعات.

I.

MIX
Papier aus verantwortungsvollen Quellen
Paper from responsible sources
FSC® C105338

Printed by Books on Demand GmbH, Norderstedt / Germany